CW00392694

SINGLE MINDING

Also by Helen Lederer

Coping with Helen Lederer

SINGLE MINDING

LEDERER ON LONE PARENTING

HELEN LEDERER

with illustrations by
Jan Lewis

Hodder & Stoughton

British Library Cataloguing in Publication Data

Lederer, Helen
Single Minding: Lederer on Lone Parenting
I. Title
306.856

ISBN: 0 340 64029 4

Typeset by Phoenix Typesetting, Ilkley, West Yorkshire

Printed and Bound in Great Britain by
Mackays of Chatham PLC

Hodder and Stoughton
A division of Hodder Headline PLC
338 Euston Road
London NW1 3BH

To Hannah and
to my mother

With huge thanks to Elinor Day who took precious time to read all my faint faxes and feed them back to me on demand, usually the same day. Without her well placed comments of 'TOO BITTER!' (and the odd tick) down the margin, *Single Minding* may well have gone further astray.

CONTENTS

Introduction: a disclaimer   ix

A personal history for the very nosey   xi

1. Getting to know your solicitor   1
2. Welcome to your new home   7
3. The debate on divorce   13
4. Morality: it's the way you tell them   17
5. How to react when it's over   25
6. Paranoia, or are you laughing at me?   31
7. A sense of failure   35
8. Loneliness, regret and melancholy   41
9. Role models   47
10. Awkward questions   51
11. Self-improvement   55
12. Childcare when you can't   59
13. Babysitting   69
14. The big reckoning: birthdays and Christmas   73
15. Have a breakdown, have a coffee morning   83
16. Compromise: a very cynical overview   91
17. Weddings: other people's   93
18. Organisation, it's a juggle   99
19. Marketing skills   105
20. Travelling light (without a wedding ring)   109
21. Holiday planning   115
22. Half term   127
23. Sex again after home alone (or home alone after sex again)   133

24. Dating blind   145
25. Bonding and bondage   149
26. There are no guarantees   155

INTRODUCTION:
A DISCLAIMER

I am glad I was actually *asked* to write a book on single parenting.

I was flattered but soon came down to earth. My only qualification for the job was that I am one.

I still wince at the words SINGLE PARENT and wish there was some other way to describe this not unusual state of affairs. But there isn't, so I've tried not to be squeamish about it.

I don't want to shock you by saying that I am white, middle-class, earn a living and so can afford help with childcare, but I might as well get it out of my system now. I beat myself up over it at times, but there it is. Being only half English in many ways, and only half everything else goes some way to assuaging the guilt – but not entirely.

In this book I have been as truthful as I dare. I have learned that people are obsessed about sex, childcare arrangements and being normal. These obsessions help us survive.

We all know there are several ways to become a single parent, I'm sure some of them haven't even been invented yet, but the list as I have it so far is: Fate; Death; Divorce; Separation; Sexuality, to name but five.

I modestly claim two of those. Fate and Divorce, and therefore I have written with this in mind.

I hope more people will write their story. Meanwhile, we have one thing in common for the purpose of this book, the rest are details.

We are all parents.

A PERSONAL HISTORY FOR THE VERY NOSEY

Sometimes I tell people, 'I chose single parenting as the best way of bonding positively with my child.'

Or sometimes I say, 'He dumped me. Bloody did, bastard.'

It all depends who I'm talking to.

People are very kind though. They will always tell you, 'There are plenty more fish . . .' Timing is all, though. I was sobbing over a left-behind jockstrap when this was suggested. It was promptly changed to 'Time heals . . .'

And it does. Eventually. All the unpleasantness will soon seem worth it. Soon you can say 'I've been there' in a knowing sort of way to others. I hate people who say 'Bought the T-shirt . . .' It's so depressing. So I won't.

But when I was 'there', I realised that all my dreams of tea on the lawn, boundless barbeques, hugely popular children, in-laws one could share a joke with, a holiday flatlet in Alsace Lorraine, double glazing . . . the works, were all quite mad. It was hard to accept at first. I'd been secretly reading my *Good Housekeeping* in readiness since the sixth form and had thought 'At last! Respect!' I'd had enough of being a fascinating free spirit and I wanted results. Which I got.

In the end I did the decent thing. I said, 'You know, there is always a door there if you need to use it.' He did. With some urgency as I recall. Love has no ties. But it does have its consequences; in my case a child. That's when I thought, 'Oh.' Then I thought, 'Shit.'

1

GETTING TO KNOW YOUR SOLICITOR

[A note from the editor of this book. She says I have to say that you don't have to be married to be a single parent. I said I knew this, and rather hoped others of parenting age would know this also.

But if you didn't know this already, sorry to worry you. If you did, and you're in the freestyle single parenting group and cleverly not legally bound, skip this chapter. Sorry.]

Visiting a solicitors' office (check the credentials before going in – they should be brown and dusty) is often the second action taken by the novice Unaccompanied Parent. The first is the primal scream.

Obviously, it will all be new to you. In my rawness I half expected to be read out a will from an old lady I used to visit when I was in the upper fifth. No doubt leaving me her secret diaries, some jewels and a rambling estate in Cornwall which couldn't be touched till I was twenty-one. Instead, I saw a few other singles like myself, all in a tizz trying to look as if we weren't. The secretaries were obviously quite prepared for this and equipped themselves accordingly. They ignored us. The fact is, only people in tizzes ever visit solicitors' offices – a bit like police stations or Brent Cross. They need help. What normal person would drop in to their solicitor's for a casual coffee and a peruse of the files, unless they were very lonely or bored with money to burn? Apart from people who think saying, 'I'm having lunch with my solicitor' makes them sound grown-up. More it means they have no friends who want to go to lunch with them and frankly I'm not surprised.

Like dentists, they tend to come on recommendation. If you ring round, someone somewhere will give you a name. They'll say, 'There's always so-and-so.' What they mean is, *they* were recommended so-and-so once as well. In my ringing round I was also offered a pelmet maker, locksmith and floor stripper.

Or just drive down any high street, and look above a Woolworths, a McDonalds or a funeral parlour. The businesses of death and soliciting are often found nestling side by side.

IT CAN BE FUN

Once inside the furry brown 'vestibule', my name was called. I jumped up from the stair I was sharing with another tizzee to be ushered into the cellar (also brown) which was wallpapered with files. A female in a suit briskly set her pinger and said she was all mine as she poised her pen over the blank A4 (soon to be my file, I eagerly supposed) ready for the gories.

GETTING USED TO IT

I began to piece together how soliciting works. First, you need the lingo. The primary use of reference will be that of 'parties'. Not the cocktail kind, unless you're being abusive, but parties meaning someone else you are talking about, often unpleasantly. It's best to stick to that, or your solicitor won't know to whom you refer.

Real names may throw her – it smacks of personal contact. All parties have ample opportunity to hone their letter-writing skills as this is the legal way of getting in touch. In fact, it's better than any calligraphy class. One really gets to see letter-writing as an art form. This would never have happened had one stayed married, so that's at least one advantage already. You write to your party, she writes to her party, they write to their parties, and he writes to his party. Never write direct to the other party if you can help it. The solicitors get huffy.

But, like all new ventures, one needs time to get the hang of things. My first reading of the other party's letter sent on to me by my ex-party's party sent me apoplectic. I took direct action. Eventually, a very irritated 999 lady pointed out that I wasn't on a hit list and no, I hadn't been sent a warning letter by a death squad. I had, in fact, received a solicitor's letter. She said the word slowly so it would sink in, and cancelled the Fire Brigade.

I felt rather foolish and re-read it. Oh yes. *Of course* it wasn't from a hit squad come to bomb my house. It was an honest-to-goodness solicitor's letter from the other side. Perfectly normal and above board. (I was pleased to note, however, that the other half's solicitor died shortly after he penned this one, which explained the delay in response. The sequel wasn't quite so Goebelesque but had a few humdingers of horribleness. He *was* trained by the deceased, after all, so I forgave him. Just to irritate the other half. Forgiveness is power – remember that in war.)

PROCEDURE: What happens next?

Link-up via letters between all parties takes place for at least a year before the first phase is reached. If the letter-writing has been agreed to be of a certain maturity and standard, the second phase is agreed upon, which is the phase before further correspondence. Eventually, on a whim, one is awarded the Decree Nisi (from the Latin, so no one knows what it means).

This is a quiet, dignified ceremony which takes place through your letter box. Once you've won your Latin certificate, you are in Go mode for the next phase of the journey, this time taking in France. The Decree Absolute. *Mais oui*! The joy of giving and receiving cannot be underestimated if you are in the hands of a solicitor.

The charges for all this are kept a loving secret until the annual invoice. Hence the overdraft.

Conceiving a letter: £50.

Writing a letter: £50.

Spelling after letter is written: £30.

Opening the other party's solicitor's letter with letter knife: £45.

Cost of cartridges for pen for signature of letter: £40.

Coffee and biscuits for in-between letter bouts: £30.

EMOTION AND LEGALITY: Can they mix?

When you first visit a solicitor you may want to cry. It's easy to be wrong-footed. This is the first opportunity to sit in front of a stranger and reveal all the injustices done to you, and you may mistake the solicitor for your old headmistress, as I did, and all hell is let loose . . .

My advice is don't do this. If it's not pub hours, buy an all-in-one gin and tonic jam-jar from the 'offy' next door and swig it down before regailing her with the who-did-what-to-whom and how many times. That way, you cut down the Kleenex time (as my solicitor cheerfully called it) and the cost. Or you can swiftly adopt the solicitor's way and 'go Biro'. Here you can learn to be brief and to the point. But nothing's wasted. My solicitor offered to forward my early letters on to Mills and Boon as she thought my essays to be right up their street (the juniors had had a right laugh, apparently), and asked me to confine my follow-up thoughts to one side of A4.

Luckily, her offices had a shredder.

PERSONAL CHOICE

Although it's easy to find a solicitor, may I say that I was particularly happy with mine during our years of letter-writing and before the Absolutement. It's best if you can get a real live wire because it can cheer you up on a rainy day, and mine certainly had pedigree. I remember the time I couldn't get hold of her for a month because she had to be on call in case *Frost on Sunday* needed her. They didn't, but she wanted to be near the studio, and I could understand that.

It certainly takes the sting out of paying the bills because at least you can say she's done breakfast telly, so she must know her stuff.

YOU DO NEED ONE

I'm afraid there are still a few repressed Bohemians who insist they can 'sort it out amongst themselves' without a 'third party'. A third party to them is a bar after midnight after they've been chucked out of the other two. They hate interference in case they're ganged-up on. Let's hope so.

They may write letters to you beginning, 'Dear So-and-So, Let's be friends and have Peace. So long as I don't have to be your partner any more, I mean.'

This 'peace' business smacks of the 60s. 'Get real' is a 90s phrase and quite apposite here, I feel.

ADVANTAGES

1. You are in good company. Any edition of *Hello!* will list the recent celeb divorces read out in any courtroom from Dakota to Dartford. Everyone is doing it. Jockeys, dart players, breakfast TV presenters. Join in the fun.
2. Partner credibility. At least people know you've done it once, so you can't have always been on the shelf or weird.
3. You can now write under 'Marital Status' on your passport 'Ex-spinster' for extra edge.
4. You're available.
   Yippee . . .

2

WELCOME TO YOUR NEW HOME

THE NICE BIT

Once the geographical boundaries are in place (by that, I mean he's surrendered his front-door key – an awkward but essential moment) – and you've got used to your new old home (i.e. you've taken your *Woman's Weekly*s out of hiding), things soon get back to normal. There is dust and talcum powder scattered just the way it used to be, and knickers can stay sunny side up until you get round to collection.

Start to have fun again. You *may* enjoy ripping or defiling some clothing he's left behind, or any historical remains of lust letters. Especially satisfying to rip up if they weren't addressed to you.

On the other hand, you *may* (but I suspect the statistics are minus ten per cent on this one) have cheerily
embraced and waved him off the premises, arranging
to meet again reassuringly soon with both your new
partners in tow, for a 'getting to know each other'
knees-up.

Either way, you are now a single unit. Tell the
authorities immediately. Less council tax to pay and
heaps of other treats in store. No flipped-up loo seats to
flip down, no stray hairs in basin, no faked fascination
during *Match of the Day* . . .

However, some readjustment is necessary, in spite of
the euphoria of the first quiet evening in. It's not that
quiet of course – it is very tiring convincing a cleverer,
but younger, person than you the reason why a bath must
be had, why the hair must be dried with a hair dryer and
not the curtains, why a party frock must not be used as a
nightie, why the duvet should not be brought downstairs
for sleeping on the sofa while watching the *Late Show*,
why they shouldn't say 'hairy bottom' and where did they
hear that from anyway? etc.

This continual series of negotiations can seem taxing
and draining at times. However, if you are successful
at meeting, say, one of these challenges a week, the
bliss of then slumping down in front of the telly with
the *Free Shopper* for stimulation and a tumbler of gin
and tonic, is indescribable. *These* are your just desserts.
Crashed out, but not broken.

Think, then, of what you don't have to do now you
are in this state of abandonment.

No breathing fire into a flagging relationship.

No missing *Brookside* because you have to tear upstairs to scrub your privates for when he comes home.

No slipping into a pressed but aired cunning sexy
number to say I'm yours but only when you've had a
nice sit down of course.

'Food and sex? Or sex and food?' you brightly quip as he hands you his coat (and sports kit if it's a Wednesday).

No putting on the interested face at the day's news, or sympathetic face at the hours put in, or fiercely supportive face at the slight made against him in the canteen queue.

Obviously, you might get a little bit lonely while adapting to the new order – but give it time.

COROLLARY to the nice bit

Then you have to sort out ACCESS (not the account). This is a word you will hear and use a lot from now on. It is a very cold and unyielding word and, like the Access card, holds an unbeatably high interest.

Many brightly coloured 'how to' books have already been written on the access thing, and one point they all agree on is this: the two erring (it's always slightly strict – one has to assume that none of the writers ever went, God forbid, solo) parents must SIT DOWN together and talk it all through.

So, if you're having a row on the doorstep, sit down. The back of the car in the drive will do – if you have a car or a drive. If you've dropped in to his work for a row on the way back from the solicitor's office, stay in the lift. Press stop and sit down. The rest of the world can wait. If you're in a pub talking it through already, move seats and sit down together again. If you have found the piece of floor either of you is dossing on temporarily at a mate's, move the sleeping bag to one side and sit down.

Then, after the sitting phase has been completed, you will have proved yourselves able to negotiate.

This can be tricky, upsetting and dreadful, so I'll skirt round this as I don't want to unduly depress myself or you. Life's too short. And it will doubtless have been shortened already by all this palava. I recommend a full head of highlights, and soon.

If your negotiation skills aren't quite up to the books' standard, don't be discouraged. For instance, you might want to: (i) Throw a beer mat, accidentally scarring his eye. It is a shame if this happens because then he'll get sympathy and you won't. (ii) Pull his hair if he has enough to make it worthwhile. (iii) Ram his car while discovering him and his new belle smugly sitting where *you* used to sit.

Don't worry, this will all pass, but it's good to have violent fantasies. One day, you won't believe how you could get so worked up over something so insignificant.

WHERE TO GET HELP WHILE YOU'RE FEELING HOT, HOT, HOT

Best contact someone with letters after their name (in any order) so *they* can tell you what to do. The books don't enhance your self-respect, which you'll need at this rather humiliating time.

You will be granted an 'audience' with a lettered expert, and once you are all sitting down you are both encouraged to say what you 'want'. Here are some examples of inner pain.

You have ruined my life.

I hate you.

You smell.

After these telling initial sound bites, you will then be referred on to someone else who is exactly the same as the first one and who asks exactly the same questions but who lives in another part of town. These experts are friends and enjoy referring cases back and forth. A bit like Chinese Whispers, or keep the kettle boiling (scald-ing) in our case.

Our second expert had a range of nods which she said would help us reach our goal of mutual under-standing. It became a game to get her to speak instead of nodding. I won. She said we were very dangerous – and I'm proud to say she looked at me while she said this. Then, having broken out of the nodding, she rattled off some visiting times and arrangements before efficiently pocketing our money. She'd done this bit (careful expressionless folding of cheque) many times before, I could see. It's a sobering thought to know you're not the first or last to pay up.

I could have suggested all these arrangements myself, but people who haven't been through this just don't realise that we are all VERY UPSET. And it takes a few years to stop BEING UPSET.

OK, if you have to be a single parent – which I accept can be a bit of an iffy one for some of the more symmetrical amongst us – you can soften the blow with a hurried 'but the child sees both of us regularly'.

Phew! No-one will thank you for it at the time, but at least the diaries in your postal area won't have had time to be slammed shut and appointments can still be made for tea and social events which require parents *and* children.

Being an outcast isn't something I'd recommend people to aspire to. So it's best, if you are the odd-one-out in your neighbourhood, to make it palatable. First, one has to understand that people can't bear to fraternise with either half of a broken couple if there is likely to be any hint of ugliness. Fair enough. Lie. Tell them you have only fond memories. Second, it's useful to realise that, although there are a lot of scared people about, *you* control the barbeque tongs.

Normal couples who split up without having children can write it off as a past mistake. And if by chance you do see him, it's easy to duck down on an escalator, disguise yourself with a goofy face or throw yourself into the guacamole at a party and stay there till the coast is clear.

But if you have a child, that's it. You can't pretend that afternoon on your rug never happened, as you could any other encounter from age nineteen onwards in my case, and somehow you have to get used to it. I am, surprise surprise, talking about this from the woman's point of view. (Did you think I'd devote a book to the man's one? Oh.) I often wonder, if I'd known ahead about the complications for access arrangements, would I have spent the afternoon on the rug? Afraid so. But would I do it again? Well, to adulterate Oscar Wilde, 'To arrange access for one child can be regarded as a misfortune; to arrange access for two looks like carelessness.' And to adulterate myself, 'Hey, each to his own.'

3

THE DEBATE ON DIVORCE

Is just possibly a waste of time. Because it's rigged. Tune in to the afternoon news, and if nothing drastic has happened that day, rest assured you will still be titilated. You will be treated to expert opinion on the current 'dialogue' – about family values and divorce.

Luckily, divorce is perennial. It's always there for discussion and particularly useful when there's nothing else to get uptight about. The debate taxing our parliamentary representatives of the people is this: 'Should it be so easy to divorce nowadays? And, anyway, wouldn't it be better for our children if they didn't come from broken homes?'

This fair and just premise is earnestly tackled by presenters who you know are either single without children, or who are deeply married and can't stop banging on about it in case anyone thought they were fat and ugly and unloved by anyone. (Fat and ugly on its own is fine but fat, ugly and divorced? Forget it – they'd find it hard to work in daytime telly, let alone the six o'clock news. Thank goodness there's a place for them on Sky – they take anyone.)

What's interesting about this debate (apart from the real-life agony, but they wouldn't want to go into all that) is the unbiased experts chosen to debate it. Mostly ex-media women who were big in the 60s but who've got time on their hands now to drive up from the country and expound the virtues of marriage and families and making jam. Or, if they can't get an ex-feminist, they find a loyal wife of an MP who's 'deviated'. She's become very keen on loyalty since she'd lose considerable perks otherwise, and it's not nice being on the other side of the tracks.

I remember the 60s. I remember Germaine Greer popping a contraceptive pill in her mouth *in front of the camera*. And I knew what *that* meant. No more being chained to a kitchen sink, being an accessory to a man, or just a wife and mother – we were being emancipated. How strange then, how paradoxical and how come, that some of this generation of women twenty years on, in linen suits and specs on chains, are now advocating marriage at all costs. Their investigations reveal that, in an obviously under-researched woolly way, divorce is rather unpleasant, and declare that children from broken (why not just go for it and say fractured, dysfunctional and not very nice) homes are inferior in every way to the nuclear, pine kitchen, bunk-beds brigade. Apart from a nutty ex-Prime Minister who believed family values helped the economy, we now have advocates of 'family' life who are the very people who questioned it in the 60s. They raised our spirits and awareness and libidinals, and now this.

Answer me this. What if the man buggered off? You can't go chasing a man with your family values if he's scarpered, can you? No.

And if that's not enough, to fuel this calm and rational afternoon telly debate they wheel in a psychologist. Her job is to produce statistics to complete the picture. For instance, inferior running and skipping abilities may well be unveiled to demonstrate children from *broken* homes – wait for it – skip less well.

And what is a broken home? A home where two adults don't live together or one where they do? Presumably the roof is a rather crucial factor in measuring relationships.

If each parent lives under a different roof, totalling two separate roofs, then they are at risk of producing children with diminished skipping abilities. But if they live under one roof, despite murderous tendencies (etc, etc . . .), the skipping thing should be fine. The debate is obviously demanding and taxing and nothing to do with sweeping poverty under the carpet and finding a scapegoat. No. Because MPs don't do it with other people and beget extra children, do they? Never.

4

MORALITY:
IT'S THE WAY YOU TELL THEM

THE FACTS OF LIFE, LOVE AND TABLE MANNERS

'You know when Daddy was your boyfriend?'

'Mmm . . .'

'Did you kiss?'

'Mmm . . .'

'Then did you go to the ball?'

'Sort of.'

'And then did you get a baby in?'

I needed assistance, and browsing through my local bookshop while waiting for keys to be cut (new nanny; old nanny had done a runner with several favoured skirts, all cash and my house keys) I determined to find a cheery and friendly facts-of-life book.

I've always been a bit grey about eggs and hair growth at the best of times, and I didn't want to pass on any confusion. Nor did I want the ex priming my daughter with 'When two people fall in love' stuff, because that isn't always true, I've discovered.

Nor could I rely on help from Topsy and Tim bless 'em. They only ever go to the library or cross the road, or go to the optician. They would be the least likely exponents of periods and sex. I needed a nitty-gritty self-catering 'This is how it is and isn't it normal and nice' book.

Harder for a child to grasp perhaps, if the two parents don't live under one roof and actively 'practise' whatever it says in the book. I found a nice, brightly coloured cover with a happy looking couple beaming at me. Their two small children were grinning out from their potties. Very primal, Freudian and married. Worse to come: a few pages in, the man looked very severe with pointy hairs on his chest, leering at his small but chubby wife and penis. Not for the squeamish. Especially when I got to the bit where they were having a chubby upside-down cuddle and the caption read 'Orgasms are like a sneeze'. What if every time I have a cold my child thinks I'm getting a baby in? So, no. There must be a slightly less graphic depiction of the birds and the bees and the fallopian tube. I moved on down the shelves in case anyone saw me and thought I was sexually frustrated. I came upon a whole series of 'how to' books. The type where whatever the subject, it's positive. 'A new baby brother or sister?

Now, this is the daddy.

Don't worry, jealousy is normal. A visit to the dentist? Don't worry, fillings are common and drilling very short-lived. Hospital visit? Don't worry, you'll get a sticker. Separated parents? Don't worry, good counselling and therapy may get you through the worst.'

I was drawn to the title 'Two Mummies'. I thought, that's me. Well, not exactly, but my ex was bound to re-group sooner or later. And at least it didn't have the chubby penis-man demonstrating fun and normality. I realised with some awe that I was now entering the 'Alternative' section. Feminists post, present and imaginary. Within seconds I fell to the floor weeping. It was so sad. I'd hooked into a completely different set of circumstances. I was so upset. The first mummy left the second mummy – one was the blood mummy but obviously that wasn't relevant. (Except I couldn't help flicking back to see if I could find any likeness between child and either mum). Anyway, when Mum One left Mum Two, Mum One kept the child for the weekends, and Mum Two had her for the week. It was *so sad*. And they were all so understanding and good to each other but, oh, the poor little thing was caught between two mummies. I got carried away and the book shop man had to pick me up from the carpet. The wailing was intrusive. He couldn't hear Vivaldi's 'Spring' I was making so much noise.

This limited literary reference made me feel even more deeply that I was alone. The books didn't speak to me. I knew I'd never find a chubby hairy man like the one in the picture and even if I did – if the cap doesn't fit (and it didn't) then I couldn't wear it.

I wanted to free myself of the shackles of a two-up, two-down, two-point-four fitted kitchen units. Not everyone can be Jane Asher. So I resolved to forget the icing on the party cake books and get real.

Perhaps magazines are more helpful. Women's magazines are only too happy to suggest untried and untested parenting tips for mugs. *She*, for example, is the magazine for 'women who juggle their lives'. So, if you don't juggle, then it's obviously not for you. But a good juggle, they say, I think, is being able to recycle your own loo paper, royally suck your partner's toe, and at the same time teach your child the complete works of Shakespeare all before the umbilical cord is cut. Preferably by you.

And more important than the facts of life, these sorts of magazines feel, is being able to 'Reinforce your child's behaviour.' They use table laying as a typical bench mark from which to illustrate behaviour. Sadly, this cuts me out of the picture. Perhaps when she's twenty she might be persuaded to help me with a gingham throwover.

However . . . when the child has laid a table-cloth upon the pine you, as the parent, are instructed to say approvingly, 'I see you have laid the table cloth.'

And then if she's put out the knives and forks, you say, 'I see you have put out the knives and forks.'

And if you get serviettes, you say, 'And the serviettes.'

And on it goes with all table markings imaginable.

As we don't have a Debenhams near us I tried the same principle at a more personal level.

'I see you're ignoring me.'

'I see you're spitting out your pasta shells.'

'I see you're looking at me quizzically.'

It didn't get me very far. Behaviour reinforcement is best used, I expect, with those parents who have table-laying equipment and normal habits.

I tried a fictitious reinforcement. I said, 'Your father and I are very disappointed at the mess.'

She looked at me.

I modified.

'Your father and I would probably both be very disappointed at the mess if he was here to see it. However, I alone at this moment in time am party to it and am communicating the disappointment in an 'as if' mode, which includes your father in principle but obviously hypothetically, as in all matters.'

I'll never know if this was useful, because she stopped listening after the word 'mess'.

The truth is, if you're a single parent you might tend to snuggle down by the telly and eat off the floor (not literally, contrary to popular fears). Not many people know that. But family ritual and huge Victorian table manners seem a little superfluous when there are just the two of you. It might have been fine for Gladstone and Disraeli and their kids, but tackling the issues of the day formally over a long table with orange juice and ketchup just feels silly.

We are far happier communing nicely at meal times on the floor. I was, however, aware that this might look a bit slobbish. So I bought some TV supper trays. A sort of Liberty print prayer mat on which to meditate your fish fingers. We did try this for a time but felt as though we were in an Argos catalogue so have gone back to the floor. But the tips do keep coming for single parents at the back section of various magazines and supplements. It's nice to be annexed, I told myself as I got down on all fours to play Mummies and Daddies, or whatever it is nowadays (single parents and MPs?), freeze my own goulash and make Christmas decorations out of panty-liners while colouring in my own home-made flash cards – all before breakfast.

On the other hand, single parenting has been allowed a bit of a strong but not stigmatised profile recently, and there are several magazines just for us! Let's hope, like most minority interest publications, they won't go bust. Well, *The Spectator* is still going, so here's hoping. Here are some of my own tips, gleaned and adapted from available material.

Cooking a stew and freezing it can be a new and

exciting area of domestic activity. Especially if you don't know your offal from your gristle. Who does? Actually I can now identify a breast from a rib or wing – because I especially like to hear the butcher say, 'Will breasts do you today, my lover? Righty ho! Not many of these in a pound!' Always makes me laugh.

Later, I discovered just how important meat is by snooping in other mothers' kitchens. One such mother spent the whole day cooking food and 'bagging it up' with anally retentive handwritten labels. That's why the kids were covered in mud, face paint and half starved when I came to collect. Also, the articles suggest flowers should be put in the day room (all my rooms are day rooms), and pillow cases must be ironed along with tea towels, pants and J-cloths.

This is for the mother with time on her hands. I found the meat mother with her head down the freezer in the garage. For one awful moment I feared it had all got too much for her – the ironing, the bagging, the flower arranging – but no. She was happily arranging, in alphabetical order, the fish pies, the meat pies, and the roulades – savoury then sweet. She was so pleased with herself she gave me some labels for my cook day. I must have appeared very grateful (stunned) because then she invited me round to dinner.

She rang just before I was leaving to check I wasn't anti-military. Only she'd got an off-duty policeman to sit next to me. The numbers, because of me being *single*, had to be *even*, and as he'd dropped round earlier on neighbourhood watch duty while she was defrosting she thought, why not?

I said I wasn't anti-anything as long as I got to sit up at the table during the mealtime along with everyone else. I didn't fancy eating out in the scullery with the dog. Once seated, she said to everyone that she just didn't know any other spare men for me. As he had to leave to get back to his wife I had to concur; she didn't. Anyway I noticed she hadn't removed the fish bones which made the plates look like the contents of a binliner. Not very attractive.

Back to the magazines.

They suggest that we utilise the old barter exchange system. This method of paying for things, while feudal in origin, is often unsung in modern times. They write, 'Imagine the scene. You are a single parent. You need some shelving, some stair protectors, and a sandpit. You don't have a husband but you do have a lover part time who is better at drilling and measuring wood than you. He knows about raw plugs, how not to fuse a house and can also sand down wood when you want that kind of look.'

Well, what would you do? It's a very persuasive argument.

I took it to heart.

For me, it started with one cooked meal for one shelf erection. Then it went to one cooked meal and a snuggle for a whole shelf erection, kitchen units and some sanding.

Then it went to one cooked meal, a snuggle and almost an overnight to collect car from the garage after it failed its MOT, make the garage pass it, knock the git down to a reasonable price because he's a man and then deliver it back all before taking child to school and getting to a job.

Or, as Sharon Stone said to Michael Douglas, 'I give good head. You re-wire.'

Or our own Delia Smith might have said, 'I give super Ocean Pie. You make TV work.'

And before people get huffy about exploitation; this system of barter exchange is a bit like marriage, but equal.

5

HOW TO REACT WHEN IT'S OVER

Quickly is best.

There's no way round this one. Prepare yourself. You are going to feel less than loving at some point. If you don't, you're lying. You're in complete denial and need help.

How can people go through the big one of selecting a partner, having a child, living together, and then whoops, it's over? Your feelings might range from being relieved to slighted or violent, depending on the level and depth of your expectations for a nice life.

But listen up; that gets you nowhere. I'm afraid men rather like that sadness. It means they can feel guilty from a distance, but loved from a distance also. The fact that someone is *upset over them* can make them feel quite chuffed. They're only human. The fact is you're on your own. And the fact is, that's a fact. Feelings will only delay getting this fact under your belt. So if you must feel – do it fast. Take a week to do the crying if you must, and then finish. Crying a lot is very unsettling for other people who at that moment don't need to cry. It also looks very primitive and unsexy. Your nose drips unpredictably, your eyes go piggy and then you go all blotched and pathetic as you pretend that you're 'Perfectly all right now, thanks.' Frankly, who is going to respect and admire you in that state? If you are foolish enough to confide in someone at work that you 'Nearly burst into tears on the tube this morning!', don't be surprised if you're subtly patronised for the rest of your working life.

Here is a helpful parable to make all this unpleasantness manageable. A woman accidentally trips over a paving stone. Whose fault was it? Hers for not looking where she was going, perhaps? Or the council's for not making it 'flush', as they say. And who cares anyway? Does she sue the council? She could, but it would take for ever, and even if there is justice eventually and she receives a bouquet of apologetic flowers from Highways and Byways Division ten years down the line, is it worth all the angst? It can't alter the gash on her shin. Only time will heal that.

Moral of this tale. Accept the facts and get on with your life as quickly as you can. Anything else will hinder your progress towards a nicer life.

You see, once a couple have separated, words are pointless. Unless they happen to love drowning in their own verbal pain, it's best to, in those immortal words, 'Let it lie.' But people don't give up easily. For instance, if you are told, 'Look, I'm just not worthy of you. You deserve someone better,' laugh loudly.

So get on with your changed life. There should be a significant amount of it left to try again. That's forty years or more of potential ecstasy, and then another twenty surrounded by loving grandchildren who dote on you . . .

It's not always easy, especially at first. But people grieve in different ways. You may be sad while he (if he's the one who has left) will be busy deceiving himself and anyone who'll listen that it's all for the best. And, really, life's a piece of cake in the long run. The clichés mount up, and soon you'll both find yourself saying things like, 'Well, in the end, when all's said and done, it's all water under the bridge isn't it? None of us are whiter than white are we, and frankly, without hope where would laughter be?' Good question and aptly put. All this on the doorstep of an access visit. Grinning from ear to ear. Or not.

'Oh, you took her to *Pinocchio* did you? *Fine.* In fact, that will give me a chance to give away my tickets to some needier people. Good. Because I had to book two months in advance for them which is why I told you we were going! Great. Well I must say you're looking tanned. Caroline all right? And the family? Marvellous!'

The man who leaves is now free to fret about, hanker after obsess about his child from a distance. You won't have time for all that if you're on the job, as it were. What luxury. But you *will* have to deal with the projected frettings from departed partner.

From friend to foe in one irrevocable step. To avoid being out-manoeuvred, I learned the step programme so favoured in Hollywood. I have adapted it for here.

Step 1. Take each day at a time. Quite easy this, since time has its own relentless certainty.

Step 2. Celebrate with a drink or a cup cake.

Step 3. Be happy about the change.

Step 4. Go back to step 3.

If you can transmogrify from horribleness to loveliness, of course you'll want to tell the world you've done it.

Divorce tends to upset society a fair amount. If you're fat, drink or take drugs, it's more or less your own problem. But if you're divorced or separated, there's a bit more of a public stigma to deal with. No fresh divorcee can say the words 'We're divorced/separated' without either an enforced defensive jollity which belies total inner pain, or an emotional choke which will make the listener remember a phone call they've got to make immediately – in another town. You soon find out who your friends are. In my case, one. Predictably, my child. She didn't seem to mind. Thankfully.

In any case, I'd never taken a roll call on my friends before the divorce, so why should I depress myself now? Our own Dessie Morris says you're only allowed three point two close friends at once – any more and you're faking it. So, at least I can rest assured that I'm one and half thirds extra genuine.

And you'll soon discover where single people are most welcome. Choir practice, because there separation is essential. Soprano and bass, and alto too, if there are some inbetweenies.

Ways of confronting separation can vary. Some people – extroverts – get very over-excited and rush to their lawyers in the middle of the night to get the first appointment the next morning. Once equipped with a legal 'section', they might put an announcement in *The Times* and generally GET IN FIRST.

'Greg and Mary are FINISHED, contrary to any rumour of reconciliation. They are totally and unequivocally miserable together. We hope they will be left in peace to get on with their divorce proceedings and generally make a mess of their next relationship, too. (Mary, you know what I'm saying.)'

It makes people feel secure to take appropriate action; i.e. the action that society demands. You do it legally; you undo it legally. It does beg the question why bother legally at all, but we're not all Bohemians, are we?

Or, you can do it secretly in collusion with each other. You might murmur to each other that, actually, it's all off. Sleep in separate rooms and not tell the children till they are thirty.

Or you can taunt your partner by pretending you are

great pals really, and that you have hardly noticed anything as ugly as a divorce has wafted by. Huh hum, you mean.

This latter approach is a most powerful weapon. I know quite a lot of dumpees who got quite used to letters turning up, written as if to a slightly distant relative with cheerful concern and approval aplenty. If this ploy is rumbled and the letters are written back in kind, they soon dry up. It's no fun playing if you've been found out.

> Dear So-and-So
>
> Thank you for the most . . . interesting marriage. It was very kind of you to shack up with me for those few short months.
>
> Do hope you are able to get out and about with no support and companionship at home. I am having great fun with all my new girlfriends. Thank you again.
>
> All the best, as ever
> Your ex-loving Ex.

Every solicitor you ever meet will always advise darkly, 'Keep all your letters.' So I bagged them all up and sent them on. They were returned. Oh you mean *not* the very early fantasy ones of doing it in the airing cupboard? Just the extremely polite and cordial and poisonous ones.

Righty-ho.

Some exes are in such deep denial they will forget they have left, and keep coming back to have showers and read your mail. Changing the locks is a suggestion, but emotions *are* tricky for some male divorcees who've not really got on top of 'this type of thing'. They are so thrown at having to be part of something bigger than a squash game they get everything mixed up. They might laugh at funerals, news of fatal illness and silences in church, and then cry at school plays, parents evenings and netball matches when their offspring may have been partially responsible for scoring a goal.

These types are unhappy with their partner's pregnancy: the hormone deposits, and the temporarily enlarged female size – being puffed up like a new sofa. Last, but not least, they will run a mile at this one: VULNERABILITY.

This pre-programmed vulnerability-at-giving-birth phase will send some men reeling. Oh, to find a non-vulnerable woman with a strident laugh who either doesn't want kids or who has already, tidily, done that.

And, if that's not enough, these men will then tell you they don't really know *what* they want. But, hint that it might be fun for you to stay around long enough to find out . . . tempting, but no.

Do I sound bitter? I don't mean to. Because being a member of the divorcee community has enabled me to be a very giving person. I've given very generously of my teapots, my boots and anything else in easy throwing distance. Only joking. I meant to say I've 'grown as a person'. And, at five foot two, there's room for that.

6

PARANOIA, OR ARE YOU LAUGHING AT ME?

When a relationship comes to an end, so will your imagination. You'll be hard pushed to think how you ever 'did it' with this person in the first place. You will look at each other and wonder how you ever wondered what they looked like naked. In fact, it's best not to. The thought may well give you a nasty turn. You've both pulled the drawbridge up and feel unpleasantly frigid. But you can't go back. You have to busily work out the next phase, daunting though it may be.

To speed up separating, this is often the optimum time for the man to play the paranoia trump card, i.e. to accuse the woman of 'making things up'. This leaves him free to depart, because she's driven him out with her paranoia.

Hence he can flee the family home, drive you mad into the bargain *and* keep a clear conscience, all because of this clever word.

It's not my fault if women are traditionally seen as paranoid. 'Neurotic' and 'highly strung' also pop up for good measure. If you further combine the words paranoid, neurotic or highly strung with the term 'single parent', you may well have people running for cover before you've unfolded your umbrella and taken your coat off. Saying pleasantly, 'Ooh, it's bitter out there!'

will get people nodding knowingly from behind their desks. How come she formed that opinion? Who spoke to her out there? No-one's accused us of being bitter before. You may earn a reputation before you've even had time to personalise your own coffee mug.

ALL ROADS LEAD TO PARANOIA

1. If you disagree with the man's point of view it will confirm that you are paranoid.
2. If you choose to ignore the point of view, it's due to paranoia.
3. Whatever reaction you choose, the reaction itself is paranoid. After all, men who've left the home still like to know they haven't lost their touch when it comes to causing a stir.
4. Pitying them for their insecurity and weakness may well be deemed paranoid, too.

I have found that doing nothing is the best reaction, as it were; but then that still gives them a thrill because they know you've made a decision to do nothing. Which in turn makes them convinced you're still paranoid.

STRATEGIES

If you have the misfortune to be hitched to a great strategist, you might find you cannot out-manoeuvre a practised manoeuvrer.

The strategist type is very clever at displacing all emotions by constantly being 'cheerful' and 'uncomprehending' of anything they don't like. This is maddening – literally. It's as if you've shacked up with a Martian. A lifetime would not be long enough to outwit this sort.

They have learned they can drive people crazy (their past is littered with letters from exes, all of whom are on Valium, thanks to him) which fills them with glee. Society at large is at risk from these types, so make sure you're not.

1. Try matching his cheeriness at the next access visit. The neighbours may well wonder why you split up in the first place, being quite so ecstatic to see each other.
2. Receiving determinedly cheerful letters from this type of ex is irritating, which is why they do it. Returning in kind can be demeaning, as you have been dictated to by their divisive ways. However, at least it's better than writing cross, upset letters. This will thrill him even more because then he knows he's wound you up.
3. If the cheerfulness fails, their next tack is 'hard done by', 'righteously outraged', or 'furiously marginalised'. The strategies are endless, and quite fruitful for any actor to study. Then just stand by and watch as they protest their innocence to any of this and accuse you of the paranoia thing.
4. Faxes are good because they don't allow room for sentiment, but they are time-consuming, which I resent. And there may be a power cut before you have a chance to reply.

The only conclusion to come to is this: the ex-partner is a completely different animal and cannot be affected by you.

SO, WHAT CAN YOU DO?

Find other people of the same species. You should know that most men are different animals from you because they don't always buy a round and they cheat at darts.

But with the right group of friends you will hear similar stories to your own, and discover that you are normal.

It is *normal* to want to ram his car if he and his new girlfriend have been spotted in it. No amount of measured cheerfulness on his part can diffuse your feelings. Thankfully, in a few weeks you will be horrified that you were prepared to do damage to your car.

One day, all this emotional charge will become highly inconvenient and disruptive, and eventually die out. (Your ex-partner won't have to wait as long to stop feeling emotional, but life is like that.)

Soon, you will be paranoid only about the important things. Such as, why wasn't your child invited to Lillian's birthday party? Was it on purpose? Everyone else had presents. Where were they going . . . ?

7

A SENSE OF FAILURE

A sense of failure is a very personal thing and should be kept that way. Don't go public on it. However, there are some schools of thought which urge people to 'share' their feelings, or else warn of the dangers of imploding. Ignore these dabbler agony aunts. Without single parents they'd be out of a job. They'd have to start help-lines on boring things like setting up a business from home or making seasonal chutney.

If there's any sharing to do – do it with yourself. Play an old tune you heard together once, look at some old snaps. Soon the penny will drop and you'll be exclaiming 'Was that really me? I wouldn't be seen dead or alive now with a man wearing a pink shirt and grey leather slip-ons.'

But, obviously, it's not *that* easy to rid yourself of that sneaking failure thing all the time. My buttons are especially pressed, for instance, when I'm stuck in a queue in a leisure park surrounded by hundreds of fun-filled families making a meal out of helping each other over the turnstile with buggies and bags, finding time to shoot the occasional glance at my own singular set-up. The thing to remember is people aren't really staring at you with pity or abhorrence, you just think they are. Unless your skirt is hitched up by the nappy-bag strap revealing some old-fashioned knickers, or you are practising your aerobic dance steps in public – it's all in the mind.

There are some bullet points, as they say in the army, to refer to when the gremlin Failure sets out to taunt you.

1. Never ask advice from anyone when you are down. You might be sufficiently vulnerable to take it. I made the mistake of asking a male friend what to do about a difficult phase in a newish relationship. He listened carefully, and then said, 'Tell him he's free to go.' Thanks to that friend, I became single again.
2. Never go on holiday with another family when you are in failure mode. Their very two-ness can incite acute loneliness. Sobbing over a sangria on a beach can be hard to laugh off. No-one will believe you've been bitten by a mosquito, and you won't be asked on holiday again.
3. Never snog anyone when you're down. Your self-esteem is so low you won't believe they mean it, and may well end up chucking them for fancying you in the first place.

Conspiracy theory. The message one gets from the outside world is that to be a family, preferably one which includes a man with a briefcase, is the *only way*. It's hardly surprising some of us allow the lack of briefcase ownership to cancel us out. Result: you feel a failure.

But let's not get hysterical. This is all very misguided. The truth is, there is no norm. Not really really. It's hard to believe at first, because the 'norms' are so keen on being prominent. They sit on both sides of the House of Commons, as well as edit the big papers and the smaller papers, run most of the advertising agencies, and are all members of the Friends of the School Parents' boards.

A single parent loses a lot of gold stars once she's been outed at school. This is because normal parents like to

revel in their highly acclaimed normality, especially at weekends – when they invite other normals to share their parties and generally commemorate normality. These parties tend to provide an 'outhouse' for the 'kids to scream and wreak chaos'. Only very confidently normal people will risk doing this.

The appearance of a non-normal, slipping through the net, can pose rather a threat. People do get very scared. But it doesn't last for long. They are the winning team, after all. They simply re-group and remind the non-normal person of their own normalness.

SOLUTION? FAKE IT

'What a lovely house/fish tank/paved-over lawn – I must get Paul/Joe/Dennis (don't say all three) to come and see it. He'd drool. But he's at a meeting right now, worse luck!' you proffer. Loving laughter followed by a resigned expression of total support and subservience. A tall order, but you can practise.

Luckily, this is the language of love. Men *love* hearing other men are at meetings. They envy them. Oh, to be at a grown-up meeting rather than a suburban 'do', squeezed on to one paving stone head-to-head with a tinkling glass and halitosis – hopefully not yours. Someone has let the rabbit out. A child has pooed in the bath, and it's all a touch out of control. Whereas a meeting represents civilisation and leather sofas and secretaries.

By the way, once your partner is at that meeting he tends to stay there; 'workaholic', you explain kindly, which is greeted by more affirmation from the envious host in rubber gloves covered in excretia. (He got the short straw – the wife was searching for the rabbit.) In fact, Paul/Joe/Dennis is still at the same meeting six months later when you meet up again at the parents' evening, but no eyebrows are ever raised.

Another feeling of failure is when your own child steps out of line. Then we really beat ourselves up and feel *perfect* failures. It's all our fault; if only we'd gone/stayed nuclear the child would be perfect like everyone else's child. Oh no. I've created a monster. Mercy me. So double penance. Even if you weren't there at the scene of the crime, it's still your fault. The old adrenal failure glands start doing overtime.

The offspring of a single parent, just like other children everywhere, might just, on one or two occasions, *not be very nice*. Other mothers may well see the single parent thing to be the cause of any trouble. These children are only four by the way; I don't think they have been taught to write VICTIMISATION, let alone PARENT PROJECTION.

Then you might get, 'What a *shame* she doesn't have a sister or brother one-point-nine years younger in tow to knock the stuffing out of her!' Ha ha! (said not laughing). 'Oh . . . you're *divorced*!! Oh well, that explains it.' A nod and a sympathetic smile.

There are various strategies to counteract such flagrant insecurity. No, I don't mean steal their window boxes, I mean shrug in a philosophically resigned way and say, 'Well, that's the way the cards fell!'

Just because they may have cream linen settees, a gingham dinner service and a home-made tree house in teak, it doesn't mean they are happy. OK, neither are you, but that's not the point.

There are endless ways to fake it, some devious, some ostentatious, but as soon as you have your tools you can con anyone that you are happy, even when you're in the temporary down phase.

1. Get a briefcase. You can shop with it, visit the bank with it, go out on a date with it because, even worn with baggy jeans, a briefcase tells the world you're one of the *haves*, not one of the have-nots. And it's handy for breath fresheners in an emergency.
2. Go get some personal cards made up. The power this brings is immediate. You place your card down firmly on a surface and it will be snapped up immediately – respect emanates from that moment forth. You can call yourself a tree surgeon, an on-line computer, an analyst, a colour coordinator, a foot panellist (not sure about this one, but I swear I've seen one) and there buys your credibility and your protection.
3. Clothes are important to disguise the inner fear. OK, if you're very much in the down phase, by all means wear the comfortable woolly sloppy joes and kilt, but give it a splash of power with a pinstripe jacket. From Oxfam branches most everywhere.

The key to remember is that everyone is scared most of the time. We are all part of the one big mess. No-one can pull rank on that one. Although it's fun to see the norms try, bless them.

8

LONELINESS, REGRET AND MELANCHOLY

ACTUALLY, YOU ARE NOT ALONE

You just have to be at the right place at the right time, and you will sooner or later hear about a set-up even stranger, and hopefully lonelier, than your own.

It's true. When you least expect it, too. I was feeling glum, flicking through some good-as-new items in a desultory sort of way – I'd just rejected an anorak still sticky from ice lolly – when I encountered another parent. I didn't panic – I showed him the ice lolly stains to play for time while I ran through my 'essential yet unrevealing small-talk topics' and got into gear. This parent helped me out. He began with rabbits. I was then able to ask about lettuce and carrots. We then switched to childcarers/minders/helps/au-pairs.

I was surprised at his criteria for the perfect nanny: 'Must be discreet,' he said. I agreed with him they should be polite, but discretion wasn't the top of my list. 'Turning up' was mine. He told me they'd had the same carer for three years. I complimented him on his obvious stability, losing interest fast as yet another perfect parent taunted me.

So intent was I on feeling inferior that I almost missed the best bit. I had to ask him to run it by me again and, being a stable kind of guy, he was happy to oblige. 'Which bit?' he inquired.

'The bit about you being divorced and then the bit after that and then the last bit twice, if you wouldn't mind.' I had settled myself eagerly on top of a bric-a-brac basket.

'Oh, you mean about the divorce settlement? Well, I can see her point up to a point. I think the point where I lost the CDs and the house was the point where I stopped seeing her point.'

'I don't mean about that bit.' I had to move him on.

'You mean about when she had me trailed by a private dick?' Did he need to ask!

'Well, she had me trailed by a dick and there were these photos . . .'

I was in heaven; this was like *The Bill* with a story.

'But the photos weren't of sufficient detail, they were taken from the estate agents and didn't offer interiors and she could only leave me on the grounds of reasonable suspicion . . .'

'And now the last bit?' I was panting.

'Well, she left me for her friend, actually, and they live together with her two children, and our discreet nanny travels between the two households.'

'So your wife, excuse me, *ex*-wife . . .' (I was enjoying the sound of the clarifications – the demoting of nuclear status was sending me into paradigms of delight), 'is now with another . . . ?'

'Woman, yes, and they seem very happy, which is fine for them, but hard for me as you can imagine.'

I could, but I wasn't going to admit solidarity, not when I had just gleaned the kind of power I had been craving ever since I was dumped myself.

'Well, I'm sure it will all work out in time. Remember, there are plenty more fish . . .' I was ecstatic – I could re-distribute the trump card I'd been dealt countless times by confirmed wives, i.e. react to my status by lowering it, then advise me to be like them, and re-marry fast.

'They're trying for a baby, and have already bought the syringe.' He gloomily selected a measuring jug and paid for it.

In that day, I understood all about labelling theory. Labels provide power. The top people in the hierarchy are understandably the most unwilling to surrender theirs.

POWERFUL: married with two children;
MIDDLE POWERFUL: divorced but remarried with new children;
WEAK: separated with no new partner or new children;
PATHETIC: separated/divorced and living happily in alternative set-up.

We feel especially good about ourselves if we can label people beneath us. All very punishing, and not community spirited *at all*. A label has nothing to do with the niceness of a person. It's all relative, and if you'll excuse the well used pun, happy families are full of relative values.

This does affect matters social. I knew the school Friends of Parents' committee needed funds and I wanted to be able to 'price up' at the jumble sale. However, as a divorcee or, worse, single parent, I was only allowed to help if I took the rejected jumble to the skip. That was a privilege compared to my new friend Jeremy. As a single parent with alternative connections, he wasn't even told about the jumble sale. Lucky him, as it turned out.

When I'd stopped feeling deliciously complacent about not being the only non-married parent in the class, I invited Jeremy to come and play. Would his child like to come, too? No, she was having fun with the other household but he didn't mind coming over for a round of Junior Scrabble. It's funny, I wouldn't have had the confidence to ask him round if he hadn't inadvertently raised my status by offering to lower his. I felt I owed him something.

However, he was a loser. Nothing to do with his status, mind, he was just a bad loser. I was thrilled with my triple word score and slept easy in my bed because of it. Alone. But happy.

On the other hand, there are times when being alone with no recourse to even a 'pretend' husband can cost you.

As Madonna is aware, it's a material world. But the absence of a partner only matters significantly when collecting your car from the garage.

Your car has failed its MOT. No man, OK, but no *car*? Further enquiry (barely concealed begging) reveals the car *may* just pass *if* it receives surgery on its underbelly. The mechanic has insisted on calling you *Mrs*, knowing full well you're not, and having blinded you with mechanical terms and problems is now saucily waiting for your reply. You say, 'Do what you have to do.' What else can you say?

Don't talk to me about buses. I'm not interested. Even though it's very important we have them, etc., etc., I'm not a bus person. Sorry. You can't escape from a party in a dignified rush and then clock the same guests as they drive past you still waiting at the bus stop a few hours on.

Anyway, you hover by the phone for results. It's good news. It's survived. You go to collect it, feeling warm and optimistic about life again. You and the buggy enter the all-male domain of Fast-Fit/Auto Mend. Although you are seen, you are ignored. Only garages operate this contradiction of greeting.

The car is finally handed over gruffly and with some distaste. Why? The sight of a woman and her handbag, let alone a buggy and a child, is upsetting for some mechanics. They don't like the invasion of territory, so it's best to be firm with them and repeat slowly and clearly

your requirements. A civil manner, a reasonable bill and, most importantly, a working car. This method is failsafe as long as you have a Man standing next to you while you 'workshop' the relationship. But male mannequins are not always handy, so it's best to get used to humiliation. At least it's better than waiting for a bus on your own.

9

ROLE MODELS

'Why isn't Daddy here all the time?' (Here we go, quick smile.)

'Because we agreed that it would be most happy if Daddy lived in another place.'

'Why?'

'Because that is the most happy plan we could think of, to make us all the most happy.'

'Why doesn't Marianne's Daddy live in another place then? Because they all live together and are happy.'

'Because some other Daddies are happiest living in the same place. It just depends what makes you the most happy. It's the way the cards fell,' I added lamely.

'Why did they fall?'

I am often asked, 'Don't you ever worry that your child needs a role model?' I reply, 'No I don't, but I can easily start if you think it would help. Why?'

And the reason given is, 'You'll need someone to balance out the female and the male.' Pardon?

Anyway, I began scratching around for some suitable candidates. I made a list. Katherine Hepburn, Germaine Greer, Darwin. Then I thought, no. They are all cleverer than me. I'd get competitive. And worse, they're all female or dead. Proper role models are alive and gender-led. That's the whole point. They have to be alive and male. How stupid not to have seen that coming.

Who would make a good role model? I looked through some pictures in the Sunday supplements for help. I saw several versions of men in ironed jeans and polo shirts and women in safari leisure wear, charmingly displaying a rowing machine or a climbing frame. The children adorning the props were clearly unaware of the part they were playing in the nuclear frame-up. They came from an agency and looked nothing like their 'parents', nor did they care.

My first choice was an ex-policeman-turned-personal trainer. He'd been recommended by a friend who'd just lost two stone in a week. She'd just gone through a painful divorce and, luckily, had gone off her food. She gave me her sessions for free so as not to waste them.

I thought he could demonstrate physical strength and play on an adventure playground adventurously. Unlike myself, who prefers to say 'Wow!' and 'Be careful!' from behind a newspaper. His conversation did bring a new dimension into our home. Boredom. Once, he said, 'Where's the kitchen?' in a very masterful way. I thought, 'Great! He's going to cook us a Sunday roast. At last we'll be catered for by a role model.' I was just about to tell him where the gravy granules were when he emerged looking very pleased with himself carrying several tins of beans. He had us doing a work-out gripping the tins to some very lewd reggae music. He had to go.

I then tried a writer friend. He was male and alive and so was perfect for the job. He seemed doubtful when I first asked him to role model for me. 'But what shall I wear?' he said. 'I haven't got a posing pouch.' No, no role model. I said, 'Just be alive and male for me, please.' Which he did.

On the first parents' evening, the teacher said, 'Yes . . . she seems . . . very . . .'

'What?' I'm thinking. 'What does she seem . . . ?'

'Mature,' she concluded.

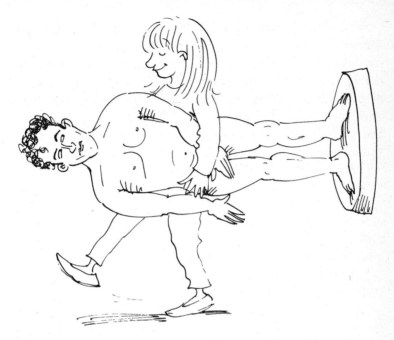

Oh no. What's wrong now. Why couldn't she be imma-ture. I wish I'd held her back. Damn.

'Yes,' the teacher continued. 'She seems very familiar with Jack Kerouac?'

My writer role model had obviously over-stepped his mark of being alive and male. He'd *talked* to her as well. Damn again.

'The staff are very impressed. Where were you *up*?'

'I haven't taken anti-depressants for about a year now,' I confided.

'No. At university.'

'Oh. Polytechnic. But you're right, it's called a uni-versity now though.'

'Mmmm,' she said, and moved on bored already.

That role model had to go, too. Why saddle a child with intellectual pretensions prematurely? Anyway, he became visibly shaken every time she blew through her straw or screamed, so I think he was relieved.

Then I remembered a family who lived in the country. They were friends I hadn't seen for years. As soon as I got there, I remembered why. We didn't get on. But I thought, check out a whole family role model; if I can't get a singular alive male to do the business, try the group thing.

'Always run when you can walk,' was the family's motto. We joined them unenthusiastically for a run on the Downs. Next, we went sailing. There we were, bobbing about on the sea being yelled at by the family's male role model to 'Ready about Leo!' I had nothing to say about Leo, but he was insistent. 'Ready about Leo' was code for swapping sides, which we did for hours. I'm afraid I then faked an appendix. I know lying isn't the best role model behaviour to offer a young mind, but sometimes needs must. I explained this doing a ton-up on the motorway. We had left in the middle of the night before any more outdoor clothes were foisted upon us. *That's* why single parents' homes can be happy, I thought triumphantly. Because no-one has to lie about being happy. Because they just are. What did I need role models for, then?

10

AWKWARD QUESTIONS

Awkward questions will only be asked in public places where the acoustics are stunning. Less revealing topics are reserved for when no-one is listening. But the big ones, How Come You Don't Live Together? and What's A Divorce? can be relied upon to come out in doctors' waiting rooms or when a new relationship is meeting your child for the first time.

WHAT TO DO WHEN IT HAPPENS

You know you're *on* when your child says 'Mummy . . .' With a sinking feeling you'll know the question is not going to be followed by a 'Where are my socks/shoes/ pyjamas?' Telepathically, you know that the smaller person's brain is delving those self-same areas you've already delved yourself. The difference in approach, though, is that, for many of us, delving doesn't help matters, it only hinders. It makes me bad-tempered, powerless and, on one unforgettable occasion, bite someone who just happened to be there, but let's not dwell. However, for your child, delving promises to provide an awareness which will make their life understandable. You can't risk repressing them. You can't say, 'Let's not talk about this until you're twenty-one'. So, roll up your sleeves and think that maybe you are playing your own small part in preventing another screwed-up individual developing, which is a service to mankind. Not least yourself. One day you'll get a thank you. Or possibly not.

I was so thorough and consistently open that, in the end, she begged me to stop. 'Can't we just have one normal day without you putting on the funny voice?'

'At least I'm being funny,' I told my shrink. She said nothing, as is her way.

Here are some examples of awkward questions:

'Mummy . . .' said in deeply concentrated tone. 'You know when I was inside your tummy . . . ?'

'Yes,' you reply, in a celebratory way.

'Did you know I was going to be me?'

'No, but I hoped you might be.' Pass.

'And when I was born, did Daddy sleep in the same bed or in the attic?'

'Well, he slept in the same bed to start with, and then in the attic later.' Good. Minor skirmish averted.

'Why did he sleep in the attic later?'

Thinking, thinking . . .

'Because he was working a lot.'

'Why wasn't he working a lot when he slept in your bed?'

Ah . . .

'Well, he had to work more later.' Surrender, and go with, 'Oh look, have you seen your Barbie dolls? I think they need to change their clothes.' But then you might add, as an afterthought for good measure, 'And also he snored.'

Child is thinking.

'He doesn't snore now, you know. At all.'

Expectant look at me.

'In fact, he's very GOOD!'

Your heart may well be breaking by now, but soldier on for there is no place else to go.

'That's nice, then.'

'He doesn't go to the loo at all either, only at the beginning like we do.'

'That's great . . . oh look, let's get the Barbies ready for a party, shall we?'

Yes, your heart's definitely breaking, but it won't be for long.

Distractions can work, but be careful not to start talking in that cheery, quick way with everyone else. It will become a habit with adults – 'Oh Graham, look at your cardigan. Is that a football team one or did you tie-dye it yourself? How enterprising! Why don't you do a drawing of one for me?'

The 'hidden agenda' to this topic – as they say in the Freemasons' womens branch – is that deep down, you fear your child must somehow come to terms with a flawed background. It's like a missing piece of the jigsaw, that you have failed to create a perfect backdrop for your child. Forget the fact that many 'perfect' backdrops might be flawed in some way. It's a pretty futile way of spending your life, trying to prove how unhappy happy people really might be just so you feel happier.

Give yourself a break. Sometimes, awkward questions aren't about your own singleness. No, they can be devastatingly awkward about *other* topics, also. Hurrah.

Once, when a waitress wearing a very short head of hair, and trousers, served us a burger, my child asked, 'Is that a man?' I explained that people have different styles of hair, including length, but the cheeriness in my voice gave me away.

Cheery voices have to be used when describing different sorts of:

Genitals,

Marital status,

Size,

Colour.

It's a minefield. The most awkward of awkward questions is usually done as a whisper. The 'May I whisper something to you?' always spells trouble. 'Why has so-and-so got hair up her nose?' 'So-and-so's very fat, isn't she?' If you opt out of the whisper and show the 'We're not repressed, are we?' mode by speaking loudly and normally, you may hurt people further. If you go with the whisper there's a chance you might alter the sentence. A slim chance. I tried to alter, 'Lucy's very fat, Mummy,' to 'Have you seen the cat, Mummy?' No-one was taken in, which made it worse. The pain, the pain.

Lavatory interest is a must for awkward questions. It starts on a roll at two and only starts to wain at thirty. Once, when I had made a grave mistake with my child about time-tabling – I told her Daddy was turning up when he wasn't, an error and a bad one but it happened – we hit the toy shop to make amends. I said, 'I know. Let's buy a baby.' 'A real one?' said she. 'No,' I replied calmly. Well, the only baby toy they had left was one which had been reduced considerably. I saw why when we got it home. This baby came with an accessorised Portaloo complete with batteries to effect a real-life flush action and fluorescent yellow urine rushing down the pyrex.

As luck would have it, it was 'Show and tell' at school the next day. Guess what we showed and told? 'It's all my fault!' I said, in what I thought was an indulgent but firm sort of way to the teacher. Am I annoying her, I wondered? Yes. I realised this particularly when she lost control of her class over our little dolly Portaloo.

So, when you've completely lost the fight, give in. Go home, stay there, take a deep breath and pour it all out. Every last drop. You'll never know what cooking sherry can do for you unless you try.

11

SELF-IMPROVEMENT

Having suddenly been changed into a single parent, like a pumpkin after the ball, you can't ignore it. It's time to do a bit more changing of your own.

I was thus inspired while sitting on the loo at the King's Head pub. I was disappointed at the standard of graffiti found on such an arty canvas, but then realised there'd been a recent cleansing. I just made out 'When the going gets tough, the tough go shopping,' which goes to show how indelible the old Flo-masters were. I thought, yes. That's me. I must go shopping.

The next weekend, my child was with her father. I paid and displayed and set out to soak up the fantasy of Shopping Mall Heaven. The assistants affirm your presence with a quiet smile, they don't care if you're a single parent or not, they just want your money like anyone else, which is surprisingly comforting. The haberdashery section offered particular delights. I was transported into another world. I lingered over zips I could never sew into an anorak. I wondered at the size of shoulder pads, even in the 90s, and sponge bra fillers (who wears these?), ending up at the strangely placed sanitary towels' section (*all* brands and two shelves long), blushing shyly. But my real inspiration for future change hit me with force at the health shop. I'd gone in to sense the disappointment of the taste of a carob bar when I noticed a display of self-help tapes. There was a tape for every problem imaginable. Sibling rivalry, nail biting, smoking, authority figures – not single parenting, interestingly. But then, who said it's a problem? I was spoiled for choice. So, to play safe, I got the lot.

For the first time in ages I was beside myself with excitement about bedtime. I switched on my 'slim-while-you-sleep' tape. A voice said, 'Now you sleep, now you sleep.' It was quite strict. Then it said there was going to be silence for half an hour while I went to sleep. Then it would come back and subliminally suggest all manner of wise things to make me perfect. Well, I was so tense in case I didn't fall asleep in time, that I got very stressed and couldn't get to sleep. In the end, I had to fast forward to get over the insomnia. The words of wisdom were, 'Don't eat cakes. Don't eat buns and don't eat sweets.' Then it abruptly clicked off, making me jump.

This had given me a taster of self-help to come. I immediately contacted a reflexologist I knew. Actually, I'd never met her but I felt she knew me. Her advert said, 'Over-stressed? Overweight? Over-wrought?' All the overs, and I thought, 'Yes, she knows me.' So, she came to my house and the first thing she said was, 'I'd better explain where I'm coming from.' I said, 'Maida Vale?' to be polite, but I wasn't really bothered. She was there, wasn't she? Then she said, 'I'm holistic.' I said, 'Well, I used to go to Sunday school but it tailed off after puberty.' She ignored me, and laid a towel on the bed. I thought, 'I'm near the phone, if she tries any funny stuff the police will be round within days. They can probably smell the patchouli oil from the station as it is. I'm perfectly safe. Then she placed a milking stool at the foot of my bed. Then she sat on it. I looked around for a cow, then I came to my senses. A cow couldn't get through the front door let alone operate the lift. Then it started. The reflexology. She grabbed a foot and what looked like a dod of WD40 and

started kneading and pummelling it as if she wasn't too happy with its essential shape. While she was digging her nail into my big toe she said she could tell that I was repressing something. Well, I had to agree there. I was repressing a scream, in case I frightened the neighbours and brought the property prices down. She said she could do a lot for me. 'Not without an anaesthetic,' I added. Or rather would have if I'd still been conscious. She said, 'You have to love yourself.' She said, 'Say "I love you".' The best I could do was, 'I'm sorry, I hardly know you.' 'No,' she said. 'To yourself. I love you. You have to say it.' In the end I said something that my ex had said to me once that I fell for. I said, 'Don't get upset, but I'm not worthy of your love.' 'No,' she said, 'Look in the mirror . . . well, all right, when you get one . . . find a bit of your body that you love, and love it.' Well I had to look carefully. There wasn't anything that stood out immediately. In fact, it was those bits that I hated the most. In the end I conceded that what I loved most were my fingernails. After all, you are what you eat. She said, 'No, try something else more visible.'

In the end I came up with two inches of my arms. 'Just from here to here,' I gestured. She was triumphant. 'Love those, then,' she said, and left.

The treatment was effective, though. I was so greased up with WD40 I slipped and sprained my ankle. £25 to say I love you to my arms, almost as good as the tapes. I tried it out, though. I said 'I love you' all the way to the chemist to get the crêpe bandage. I made a lot of friends that day. Anyway, she did leave me some crystals. She whipped them out of her Peruvian holdall. I think she expected me not to notice they were just pebbles. Which I didn't. I said, 'What do you do with them?' She said, 'You pay for them. £50 a throw.' Did I want a happiness crystal, a love one, a get-as-slim-as-a-pin one or be-hugely-popular one? Which? Unfortunately, she didn't have a for-Christ's-sake-make-a-decision-for-me crystal so I got the lot – luckily she took Access. Even luckier, there was no money in it.

But don't be put off. There are many more successful paths to self-improvement at this exciting time. The biggest improvement is that you are not accountable to anyone (yet). You can clean out a whole jar of peanut butter with your fingers while watching Oprah, and no-one would ever know.

12

CHILDCARE WHEN YOU CAN'T

This is a fascinating and gripping topic for people everywhere. Whatever you're doing, whatever the circumstances, people will demand, 'And who's looking after the child?' People *need* to know about the child who isn't there rather than the person who is. You must be held accountable. And this fervent curiosity about other people's childcare arrangements is catching.

This is because, underlying all the perfect arrangements in the world, there still permeates the belief that a woman's place is at home with her children and she shouldn't be dilly-dallying with a job in the first place. Even women who run nanny agencies for working mothers get cross because you are out and about in the workplace and don't return their calls. A double standard or what?

I mean, how do successful, rounded high-flyers (or indeed dysfunctional headcase high-flyers) sort out their infant surveillance? How do they manage to skip happily off to the office or film set or Homebase without a care in the world? How can they turn up for impromptu drinks on a whim from a chance encounter at bath time, bedtime book time or being sick in the night time? How do they remain smug in the knowledge that their child will be picked up from school on time, be taken to the right child for tea, have a full social diary that any PR company would die for, arrive for the piano lesson across town in the rush hour having practised ceaselessly without training, won the ugly duckling life-saving award due to hours put in at the lido (which the mother wouldn't be seen dead in) and generally be an active participating doer and shaker of society *without* the mother lifting a finger? (Except to dial the shopping, the take-away and the carpet cleaner.)

How, how, how? Here the desperation starts on a roll and builds horribly. How does the child get whisked to the doctor at the first sign of any malady or even before, how does the child present itself as a washed, sunny, loving child when guilt-free mummy sails in slightly pissed and ready for another? How come the child doesn't go into screaming punishment flaying-limb mode, but instead inquires sweetly about the mother's day? You can see the problem.

Perhaps this is just how it seems from the outside. Perhaps their children leave home at the earliest opportunity and are cruelly accusing of their parents in later life, causing remorse. Let's hope so. Or perhaps, if you're hugely rich you really can buy childcare successfully and just live for the now. *Or* if you have to earn a living and have childcare you just get on with it – which seems the norm. I have to confess I can't talk about this one without worrying. The compromise does not sit happily and we all get very uptight and defensive when describing our 'arrangements'. Basically, a better system of guilt-free, happy childcare hasn't been invented yet. Perhaps Microsoft will lead the way here, as in other fields. Whichever group you're in: Rich, Ordinary, Poor, somewhere along the line you may encounter the zone of NANNY or share a childminder or au-pair or any odd person who wants to do it as long as they're paid. This is a club you join, if you can afford it, which changes your life. 'Learn as you screw up' is the only way forward, because no-one will tell you the rules.

Nannies are very powerful. Like Virginia Botts they can withdraw their services just like that, with great consequence. So, employers of nannies have to keep them sweet. There is no ceiling to this. You have to keep this up for ever. One drop in standards and all your investment is down the Swanee. Just because you gave the nanny the kind of birthday present *you* would secretly have liked to have been given does not mean a week later you can ask for an extra half hour's work and get it with good cheer, even if you have hired another head-hunted babysitter (£15 per hour min.) to relieve her at 5.05pm. The street value of that birthday gift drops off the face of the market and you are in the red. Never get angry and indignant. There are two sides to this relationship and yours doesn't count. The nanny is always right.

You see, the nanny phenomenon sits outside normal social exchange mechanisms because you need them so much. There's no give and take, because they can leave

and you don't want them to. Unless you hate each other, of course, and even then you must secretly have found someone else to take over. Two-timing is hard when your phone calls are monitored by the nanny. And, anyway, some nannies like to hate their employers. It gives them that extra energy spin we all strive for. This game is not for the faint-hearted.

Let's just say, hypothetically, you get something right and end up with a nanny who seems to like both you and the child. It can happen – think of the lottery winners. One will be naturally desperate to hang on to this equilibrium of domestic cheer and harmony for as long as possible. Now the problem with time passing is that although time heals (apparently), your children will, with time, have to grow up. Whereupon the nannies turn tail and wander off in the direction of other peoples' littler, cuddly chubblies. Here, they can impose their own will and ownership on dependent, malleable charges. Much more fun than picking up the child from school and doing homework with little adults who are unpersuasive and less tactile and are at risk from growing more like their mother everyday. Heaven forbid.

Although, it must be said that nannies have great influence over their charges. Particularly in intelligence and general language acquisition – forget genetic determination. My child learned to say, 'That's it, I'm leaving,' before she was four, as well as quoting the complete works of Take That and Prince and knowing the best clubs to go to in Brixton without getting strip-searched. Which, I should imagine, will stand her in good stead sooner or later.

Wouldn't it be preferable to have a Mrs Beeton type on wheels, or even a Mrs Beeton type live-in (you could partition-off the siting-room wall with a screen and provide a comfy corner with slippers, a sewing box and a Teasmaid). Someone who said things like, 'Have a lovely time,' to you, or, 'How did it go?' in a smiley and genuinely interested sort of way. If such a nanny type exists, you can bet your dollar she's the only one in your area and she's been bagsied.

To keep the nanny that you like you might try and lie about your child's age so she doesn't have to go to school, or hire a governess so the nanny has no apparent reason to move on. Or you might pop out another child pronto (if possible) before the nanny has time to phone her international agency about another placement. You can plan the nursery together and pay her full whack during the gestating nine months, just to ensure she doesn't go off with another single parent or, worse, to a new nuclear placement, which would be a double blow and cause for unsightly envy.

The next stage in the nanny/au-pair/whatsit game is to resent what you are paying out in wages/fees for a job that you could be doing yourself but which you're not doing or aren't able to do. To deal with this you might get a bit cocky and think that you can beat the system with a NANNY SHARE. Be careful. Just because it's very popular with the middle classes who want to keep their costs down but can't bear the thought of a 'live-in', does not mean it's the ultimate system.

IT'S A NANNY'S WORLD

A system of Nanny's choice operates. They choose their employer, they choose whom they will share their employer with and they choose when to leave either or both. But first, they will receive instruction from the nanny's governing body, otherwise known as the Nanny Teas.

Nannies take it in turns to host a nanny tea. About half a dozen nannies convene at an employer's house, having parcelled up their charges and packed their crisps and the odd lager in the nappy bag. Here they take a moral inventory of which employer has the nicest fabrics, cars, Impressionist paintings, tacky prints, hair. The babes are expected to sort out their own wars on the climbing frame or in the paddling pool. If a mishap occurs and a 999 is needed, the house owner's babe is always routinely blamed for not being able to 'share' its toys, and is hence responsible for any maiming or injury incurred.

Once they get on to the psychological make-up of the mothers, hatred, resentment and grudges are all pooled in the nannies' coven. Intentions of notice giving are all confirmed as they wave goodbye to this particular nanny oracle and stagger into the Range Rovers with their charges and any empties.

If a nanny has nothing to do between nine and three-thirty while one child is at school and the other is sleeping, they understandably get bored and may start stealing your clothes and phoning Australia for a lark. Who wouldn't? This is often the time for a mother to hook into another mother and – ha, ha – 'dovetail' arrangements. That's how the agency describes it. The Dovetail.

The plan is a con, but a lot of mothers are taken in. Pay less and keep same nanny? Sounds like someone is on your side all of a sudden? Check it out. The mother applies to an agency or a notice board (concealed under the used wordprocessors and French lessons for tots). The two mothers then have to fit together like a glove on a *share* basis. I've taught myself to laugh at the word 'share', which saves on stress. Many's the time I have only just resisted hiring a hit man to flour-bomb the other mother's home. 'Share?' I cry maniacally. 'Share? Get me a gun. I will eradicate injustice and horribleness from society, but Nanny Shares must be outlawed.'

A good tip at the outset is never to share with another mother whose name ends with 'ena'. This can be Selena, Farina, Georgina, Helena, Thumbelina – anyone from that class is a threat to mankind and superbly skilled at manipulating the already complex nanny personality type to her advantage. These mothers order the nanny about. They list errands, duties, essential jobs and never smile or treat the nanny with interest or pleasantness. This is rewarded with warmth and respect. Weird or what? If you, on the other hand, treat a nanny as a person with feelings and sensitivity they think you're a div, a nurd and a prat and put you on the agenda for discussion at the next nannies' tea.

So, if you are between jobs, the best gap in the market to exploit is dumped mothers. And, for once, I don't mean by a man. That sort of dumping has to come before the nanny dumping. Set up your own nanny share agency. Get on top and get your own back. You can be a legal madam and pimp your revenge on the 'enas' of this world. Really posh high-flyer mothers are reduced to gibbering no-hopers when they run to an agency, so get them while they are dependent and desperate. (The nannies are taught how to use this trump card at the nanny tech, or wherever they learn their manipulation skills.) These mothers' powerbase has gone up in a puff of baby talc. Their nanny may have gone off to another, proper family, or perhaps she's ventured into the share zone and is being crippled by the brusque other mother. They snivel into the phone saying, 'It's not *fair*. I asked her to take the washing in and the other mother kept her late and now I haven't any clean pants for my meeting tomorrow. Could you possibly intervene because I'm desperate and I just can't communicate in case she makes me cry.'

If you're feeling altogether less dependent, get an au-pair. But how can you replace the nanny your child loves more than you with another person who may not speak the same language? She probably prefers the Tower of London and the Planetarium to going crazy on the swings.

At least as a single you won't find the au-pair in bed with your partner, or if you're really posh be murdered by him, but you will have to share the loo, start wearing a dressing-gown and pretend you are a nice person *all the time*.

So, I have to get up even earlier to work, so I can pay the nanny, so I can go out to work in order to pay the nanny full-time even though she's part-time in term-time although she isn't now because I have to work nights as well so I can pay her full-time so she will stay with us.

By the way, never discuss all this in mixed company, i.e. people with no nannies. They will either hate you for having one, or they will just feel nauseous anyway. The scrape of chair legs is inevitable as soon as the word nanny slips out. You could try lying. I used to say my child was looked after by a friend for absolutely no money at all, but everyone knew I was lying. Certain TV presenters and actresses can get away with it, but I'm not in the same league. I've noticed that people without children mostly get quite expert on this and suggest you read *Family and Kinship in East London*. This is deemed a good example of extended family caretaking, whereby if society does its job there would be no need for Nanny or childminders – everyone would be breast-fed by aunts and uncles alike. I've never been able to draw from this, having had most of my extended family done in during the war before I was born.

Also, don't bring nanny troubles up with the 'ena' brigade. They invariably claim perfection with their own system and will be at pains to point out the intricacies of their care arrangements. Something to do with a nanny flat, skiing opportunities and a clothes allowance. The scrape of the chair leg should legitimately be made by you in this case.

BEWARE HOW YOU CHOOSE A NANNY (IF YOU HAVE ANY SAY AT ALL)

When one is newly alone one is also prey to nannies who happen to be stronger than yourself. Why wouldn't they be? They are not in your shoes. One nanny gave me a reference to her madam at 'Little Tops'. About me she said I was 'volatile'. This was true, as it happened, having been freshly left with a babe-in-arms at the time. This nanny came with a boyfriend attached at the hip. He didn't actually pass the interview because she sensibly left him outside on that one occasion. She was better at the interview than me. I forgot to ask some helpful questions. Did she like wearing my clothes, for example?

She told me she had a pager 'because she took her job seriously.' I was so impressed I forgot I was hiring a nanny and thought momentarily I was hiring a despatch rider. She got the job and so, inevitably, did the boyfriend.

I'd come home and find them entwined on the sofa. They'd complement me on my choice of freezer items.

In the end they had to go. The child will thank me for it one day. I hope. What's wrong with Mary Poppins? Apart from flat feet?

13

BABYSITTING

'I couldn't get a babysitter!' is a familiar cry the world over. But not one to be overly used in normal conversation. Because of its drudgery quotient – dependency factor ten – no-one will want to talk to you about being weak, boring and reliant on other people. Sad, but true. All right, the husbands may fake an interest in the wives' detailed account of how difficult it was to get one and would you mind driving the babysitter back to Wales tonight, she's staying with her aunt, so don't drink will you.

If this topic of childcare rears its head, people will invariably wander away pronto. While having a family life is considered very nice and all that, the actual day-to-day childcare should simply 'unfold' – that's all anyone needs to know. Otherwise, it's like watching *Jimmy's*. We know operations are necessary but they're not quite nice at supper time.

But it's worth looking at the bright side momentarily. Not having a babysitter is the ultimate excuse to get you out of something horrible. No need to tax your brain – or maybe even your conscience – with a tissue of lies. All that's required is a phone-call saying, 'I can't believe it. Janet's just rung, she's got flu! What can I do?' You are hopeless, hapless and privately ecstatic. Who could mess with that? No-one would dare encourage you to leave your precious lovely to the mercy of a house fire, a gas explosion or court summons. Not only do you get out of the gig, but you get sympathy as well! A person without the babysitter alibi has no such facility, and is looked down on for lying deceitfully, while you get out of it with a blessing. In fact, it's such a fail-safe alibi, single people with no children sometimes try having a babysitter crisis. This is nearly always rumbled.

I remember when I was new and green to the game. I was newly dumped, occasionally wanted to go out but also wanted to do the best thing for my child. My first forays proved expensive. I applied to an agency. Luckily they accepted me. I was so relieved to be of 'good report' that I happily handed over a huge cheque. I was then supplied with several nice young girls to do the job. They had all been selected and vetted to a standard the FBI would be proud of.

The only proviso I added of my own after all that vetting was that they were to read bedtime stories and not my mail. This must have got confused in translation via the agency, and time and again I'd come home to a room full of opened letters and ripped envelopes with a screaming child deprived of *Spot at the Farm* again. Or maybe they were just nosey.

All this endeavour was my way of ensuring that my child would never have to have dealings with the kind of babysitter I once had to look after me. Yes Susan. You know who you are. I was ten, and sporting what I considered to be a most prized fashion item. A plastic leather-lookalike jerkin. This I wore with pride and excitement. I bounced into the sitting room to be greeted with gales of shocked laughter from Susan the babysitter. I looked behind me. No, it was definitely me who was the source of mirth. I checked my appearance. Yes, I was wearing clothes, so it couldn't be that. Or could it? Oh, my jerkin. She's laughing at my jerkin. I raced upstairs to the box room and stayed there until

Susan was sufficiently contrite on her knees, and my sister had raided enough plunder from the larder to entice me downstairs to an all-night TV vigil – to compensate for hurt feelings.

You will always need a babysitter sooner or later, and if you are fortunate you may sometimes get one. So, it is worth getting it right. It helps if they have their own cars – and for that registration fee most girls should be driving Porsches at least – otherwise you have to wake the child up to drive them home which is tedious. Or you can fork out for a 'cosi-car' to send them home – that's after forking out for their fee, the agency fee, the biscuit barrel fee and any shampoo or other sundries used on the job.

Sometimes I ask my mother to do it. But because she's extremely old and might drop the child after a whisky, she's only allowed to do the first shift, and I get a babysitter girl to do the second shift, keeping costs down but blood pressure up due to planning and dependency. What if one doesn't turn up? My mother's been known to cancel at the last minute – bridge waits for no man, especially if you're playing for CASH. You have to have contingency plans, but after all that original planning I'm finished and so leave the rest to the gods.

I know I haven't got it right. All I need to do is meet the perfect person. She will live nearby, and be available at the drop of a hat to babysit to our hearts' content. Other people seem to know such *Tante* Poppins, but I don't. I stand for hours with a pencil and pad in front of notice boards in childrens' shops. I jot down names and numbers of babysitters offering their services. It's compulsive. While I'm there I get distracted and start wondering if I wouldn't rather have my portrait done in lithograms instead, or train as a Montessori nursery teacher in my spare time.

In the end I put one up myself. 'Babysitter available – with baby.' I thought it might encourage me to knit while I sat – and help pay the tax bill.

14

THE BIG RECKONING:
BIRTHDAYS AND CHRISTMAS

A PHILOSOPHICAL INDULGENCE

It's funny. You can go through life – well a whole week max – feeling completely happy. Perhaps. And then, like Proust must have done, walk past Bartons the bakers or a Patisserie Sangee Nangee and get a whiff of a marvellous McVitie's macaroon, or a madeleine even, and in two shakes of a reminisce you can be transported back to a place in your past. (A sniff of BP supergrade also does it for me, but I'm over-stimulated.) This sensation will trigger memories of your childhood which will most definitely be a BIRTHDAY or a CHRISTMAS. *This* is how important the day is. And you alone have the responsibility of enforcing perfection on this family-oriented day for your child.

Before you dive for the Valium, remember, you mustn't let the power of long-term memory make you nervous in your own ability to provide a humdinger. Nostalgic reminiscences of your own will only get in the way. You mustn't feel bereft because as a single P you may not be able to do to your off-spring what was done for you. In many cases this will be a blessing, but I digress. I told myself this as I was frozen with fear as the first of twenty children bounded up to my door expecting at the

very least a Bit of a Bash on my child's fourth birthday. Had I got enough parcels wrapped up? Could I manage the sound system for Pass the Parcel and not leave people out or, worse, stop at the same child each time and cause grief and indignation? Could I get the tea ready and stop my child having a disappointment tantrum, and mop up the mess where someone had spilt Ribena on the carpet before the mothers saw it, and look in control?

That's why I nearly didn't let them in. I remembered how it was the year before. No whimsy nostalgia there; only the cold shudder of truth.

As I am of the pre-Beadle camcorder generation I'm more familiar with the ritual of the buzz of a projector in a darkened room with unrelated images of the past jolting across a door handle, than of people falling into paddling pools or getting caught on barbed wire. I was forced to watch one such accident-free cine reel two Christmases ago. There I was with my sister, surrounded by two loving parents, one mowing the lawn and the

other serving tea on it. We wore corduroy dungarees
and had a little push dog on wheels and seemed to move
very joltingly. Cine film does funny things to one's gait,
or else I have since corrected a limp. We all were smiling
at a hefty birthday cake, looking madly at the camera. In
my bitterness I tried to create a ripple on the surface of
all this happy family movietone archive. Why was Dad
always mowing the lawn? Who always baked the cake?
Didn't they ever argue? They didn't. Oh. I made up for
this by watching *Brookside* omnibus for family reality
on film. At least they get to quarrel.

Just because all your childhood birthdays may have
been spent with a totally happy family of two parents,
uncles, aunts, jackdaws, the lot, you don't *have* to provide
an identical backdrop for your own child. Unless you go
to an extras agency and pay through the nose for happy
smiling party guests as well as a Sony video recorder,
how are you going to do it? You must invent your own
meaningful ceremony which has dignity and aplomb.

If it's your own birthday, be prepared. Presents can be
a stickler. Especially if your child is too young to go to
Woolies unaccompanied, and the ex is too unimaginative
to do it on your child's behalf, and the childcarer is in a
huff with you and would love for you not to have any
presents at all. In these cases, swallow your pride and
give one to yourself. The same for Christmas day. And
Mothers' day. And Guy Fawkes day, and PMT day.

And don't meander back to birthdays past, when you
had thirty-seven candles on your cake as opposed to
thirty-eight the following year. That's not nostalgia;
that's masochism.

Think of a creative birthday for your child. Go to an
adventure playground and have an adventure. Bump into
a policeman who says you've double-parked. Have a row
on purpose and take the kids for a tour of the police
cells. Have a few colleagues round from the nursery for

drinks and nibbles from an experienced caterer (me). Get the children to come on afterwards. Or grit your teeth and get the ex partner to come over. The smile on your face can be unpicked at bedtime. Along with the tail on the donkey and the chewed sausage on a stick.

You can have a laugh at the thought of him doing his party the following day. Rituals often come in duplicate so make sure yours is good. No-one has beaten the police station theme yet.

But, no matter how bad a birthday party can be, nothing can compete with the Christmas period. This is the mother of all days of reckoning. It lasts from the day you buy your advent calendar to mid-January when people finally stop saying 'Are you coming to us, or are we coming to you?'

This usually rainy season is bad all round, especially if you're facing it newly alone. In fact, it's so bad it's worse than several other pretty bad things. It's worse than flatulence in a lift with you and one other person that you know slightly; being last in the mothers' sack race and still smiling gamely when you trip; not locking the loo door properly to be interrupted by various relations concerned about your humming; using an old frayed tampax as your roller-ball to sign an overdraft agreement; having chewing-gum inexplicably planted unbeknownst in your nethers and then having to extract yourself from said pants in the gym changing room.

Yes, all this does happen, but even collectively it can't compete with the Christmas period. Instead of singing 'Away in a manger' you will be singing 'Away with the fairies, I-I-I ha-ave no friends, Who are single and lonely, I-I-I've gone round the bend.'

But stop a while. Remember, this is all a plot. Primarily set up by Gordon and Fraser and other major wrapping-paper companies. It's their big time. Spare a thought for them. Without Christmas, where would they be? Bit by bit other shops join in, even churches, until the message is up and running. CHRISTMAS IS A FAMILY TIME. ONLY FAMILIES NEED APPLY. This six-week family period is a time of preparing to give Pifco combs and Baywatch posters and gardening gloves to each other before sitting down together to worship a great big turkey. Without killing each other. Only the turkey must be dead.

Methods used by kidnappers are employed. Posters and videos on a loop inside stores, as well as relentless and repetitive adverts depicting families opening presents together penetrate our purse. Everything must be sold, from plate-warmers to coathangers to nail scissors. As long as it is a two-point-four-children family ripping open the merchandise, and there is a holly leaf on the price tag, we're on course. One is never shown a person in a bedsit opening her single platter of turkey and two veg for one from Tesco's. Even though Tesco makes 'em. These people aren't targeted for Christmas, out of mind and hopefully out of sight. I can quite see why, loneliness has never knowingly sold anything.

And if you haven't been successfully ousted from the high street precinct, you will definitely feel the pinch on the drinks parties circuit. This grouping and re-grouping in the same people's front rooms doesn't let up until all the Alka-Seltzers, rescue remedies and morning-after pills have been consumed.

So let's just suppose you were happily adjusted/reconciled/on top of your life before Dec. 1st, by Dec. 2nd you will be frazzled, alienated, alone, exiled and mad. Everywhere you look there will be persistent, indelible reminders that Christmas is a time for happy people. For children and families to celebrate. To celebrate what? It's so long since anyone mentioned Jesus you could be forgiven for thinking he's someone's Spanish pen pal. The words 'drinks party' or 'drinks do' (these are worse) will be on everyone's lips. So much so that you will find yourself buying a ton of mince pies, just in case someone drops round.

(And I don't mean Him. He doesn't get offered a sherry before he takes your life blood away – well that's how it seems at this crazy, emotionally haywire time of year. It would be nice to be with your child, but you have to *share*, he reminds you. Bother.)

It's like the war. People panic buy. They are programmed to believe that, although someone who is supposed to be our saviour has been born (which seems on balance a nicer thing to celebrate than twenty years of *Blind Date*), more importantly the shops will be closed and we won't be able to buy anything ever again. Or at least for one whole day. So people grab salt, matches, light bulbs, as well as the festive fayre. Turkey, sprouts, sausage meat, almost any consumable which reliably makes you fart.

The only turkey I ever cooked was a natural one. It was naturally killed as well. The butcher told me, they talked him through the impending trauma and hoped he didn't shit himself just before curtains. The turkey (Lawrence, as he affectionately became known) was very prominent. So prominent he wouldn't fit in the fridge, or even the oven, I discovered on Christmas morning, so he had to be autopsied into pieces. Because he was a Friends of the Earth type bird he had a natural way about him. He let himself smell, and was confident in his appearance, hence avoiding leg or pubic waxing and other such trimmings. I, carefully watched by the child, lit a Christmas match and burned off unsightly stray pubic hairs before finally douching him with a fragrant turkey freshener for his internals. Not a success. Pink meat, still visible pubic hair and pungent stuffing. (The worst kind of sex, I'm sure you'd agree.)

So, once you've done the nativity play, readjusted your mascara and sung the carols without sobbing too noticeably, you can do the cards. I send them out the same day I receive them, having phoned the person to get their address because I can't find it in my address book. I then think, what's the point? There is no point in sending a card to some you've just spoken to on the phone, and no point in speaking to someone on the phone you weren't going to send a card to until shamed into doing so.

Right. The cards are done. You've pinned up three and lost the rest. (Well, that's what you tell people.) The wreath is nailed pagan-like on the door in all its glory. There is a lot of competition on wreaths. It seems to represent death and people can't get enough of it at Christmas. Anyway, anything goes on a wreath, it seems. Last year it was all walnut and limes, I then glued on some little red Edam cheeses to be different. Next door copied. I then found some wooden salt and pepper mills that looked nice dangling down off a coat hanger. Next door copied, but added a string of onions. Annoyed, I blew up some pretty multi-coloured condoms I'd been saving for the tree and hung those around the cloves and tartan bows. Next door took theirs down. Hooray for Christmas.

Now, it doesn't matter if you haven't crashed eight different front-room dos and sampled the full range of various supermarkets' mince pies. Just surviving one do with a cheery look on your merry face while your child asks when can you go home is a coup. I grant you there won't be much there to hold you both. All the under forty's are fifteen and shooting up in the TV lounge, and the over forty's are wrestling with the Christmas finger fayre. They'll be blowing icing sugar at you and spitting out mincemeat while persisting with a Christmas anecdote which they've told so many times they're boring themselves. On these occasions, when someone suggests Charades, it's best to have a burst pipe. Or to offer the hostess a sanitary towel. Even if she doesn't want one, tell her it will help the mulled-wine stain on their new fleck. While she's freaking out, you can quietly slip away. Unnoticed.

That's nothing compared to the mighty thorn called ACCESS AT CHRISTMAS. You might as well say Hitler had a point, it's so controversial. All that propaganda you've been resisting till now will finally settle. The expectation of family life has become so disproportionate, you can only see in fours. You find yourself laying out four places for breakfast. Yourself, an imaginary husband, your child and a sibling. You reminisce to your imaginary family around the imaginary fire about imaginary Christmases that never were. Forgetting the tears, the rows, the slightly sozzled Father Christmas who fell over while putting presents on your bed and gave out American Tan nylons instead of toys. No. Christmas is a time for families and snow and wine and Cliff Richard and tears of happiness captured in a family tableau in front of the tree. You are attempting this uncomfortable scenario when the doorbell goes and you have to stretch to get rid of the pins and needles. It is time for your child to be taken to join just such another tableau, but with different personnel. (Mine are more fun, I smugly think, but then I would.)

In this event a 'buy-out' of access arrangements to cover all Christmases is wise. This can serve as a reference for all ensuing international treaties until offspring tells us both our services are no longer required. The buy-out should read thus:

He leaves you – you get Christmas day.
You leave him – you get Christmas day.

Signed and sealed in the presence of officials, i.e. me.

Trouble is, there's Boxing Day. The most dreary day in the calendar, apart from Easter Monday when the shops are closed and you can't buy petrol or Flora. So he might as well have Boxing Day. Expect him to look hang-dog, but it's just a day for God's sake, you tell him. Heated-up turkey tastes just the same. If I know men (I clearly didn't, but I'm learning) on the day itself, they will tuck themselves in obtrusively with another family and a turkey and a drinks do. The hosts will be thrilled to have an extra man to show to their community – how exotic, people will say.

So he's fed and watered and raring to go for a great Boxing Day, while you surrender the last link with real life (given the eroded state of mind you're in) and settle down to a lonely Boxing Day with no-one to play Happy Families or Donkey with.

Remember, there must be others in your shoes. Not everyone is a vital part of a drinks do. They can't all be in a National Trust bothy in the Cotswolds building snow-men and tobogganing with tartan scarves on. Remember whenever you are alone, someone else is, too. This gives me great strength. I spend Boxing Day evening by myself knowing I'm not alone because a lot of people are doing the very same thing. I just haven't met them yet. But I know that, when I do, we'll already have that in common. Post Christmas stress for single parents.

So, I have a·bath, drink the sherry and watch telly, talk to myself, talk to an admiring Melvyn Bragg about my life and loves, hand back the damehood and give all my money to charity. Then I do some sit-ups for extra virtue, or have a boiling bath with a pumice stone rub-down – which gives the best rush of blood imaginable – and I'm as right as rain.

What makes the new year so exciting and full of possibility and hope is that we are not in the festive period any more, so that's something to be merry about.

15

HAVE A BREAKDOWN,
HAVE A COFFEE MORNING

Once you are a parent, you'll discover coffee mornings. At first, the concept may appear to be a bit repressed and middle class. You might, for instance, prefer the elevenses idea – a bourbon and a spritzer if it's raining, or a mini roll and a lager if it's sunny – I know I've always been flexible. But a real coffee morning can help in your pursuit of happiness, normality and comfort. And, more essentially, it gets you over that danger-zone time in the morning – whether, as a single parent, you're still getting used to the idea of being alone or, having got used to the idea, you're still in need of getting through the morning.

I have to say, mornings are the worst. Anyone who has been even the slightest bit depressed will know that waking up can be *bad*. There's something about sun-up which, although peaceful, is too quiet. Oh for some noise! Even next door's electric organ playing 'Food glorious food!' would be welcome right now.

In this state, you might easily forget you were ever in your life invited round to someone else's house for coffee. Never fear. Help is at hand. Reach out for your radio. The sound of human voices will remind you that, while you lie alone, panicking about your life, there are a group of other people sitting around a microphone all

panicking about theirs. One may be panicking about
the film they've got to talk about but haven't seen,
one may be asked to comment on their government's
policy and they don't know what it is, another may be
chairing the whole thing and panicking because he's
got diarrhoea and has to keep leaving the 'live debate'
to find a loo. But they are all joined in one general
fellowship of panickers. The difference with these people
is that, while they panic, they can also bluff. Follow their
example. Combine with a coffee morning, where no-one
admits to panicking. That's why they were founded – to
provide a panic-free fellowship.

The first question about coffee mornings on everyone's
lips I'm sure is: will there be one near you? Typically,
we think of coffee mornings dominating areas like
Weybridge, Edgbaston and Morningside. Places where
men have umbrellas and prefer to work while their wives
dust and doodle. Don't be prejudiced. You can make your
own coffee morning happen, but it's best to start by being
a guest at someone else's. To learn what's what. Then
the world's your coffee cup.

At first, it may feel like being invited to a tupperware
party, without the tupperware. But if you open your eyes
you will see the coffee morning as a sort of Ashram
for the spiritually let-down. As soon as you enter
another mother's kitchen your senses will be pricked.
A different Pledge flavour perhaps, or a different Glade
odour emanating from in the bathroom. Even a different
perception of taste in kitchen decor. Who knows, I'd
never have thought of stencilling cherries on my tiles,
kettle *and* toaster. As soon as your chime has been
answered you will be affirmed. Kettles will be plugged
in, mugs will be filled and fig rolls (if they're mean) or
jaffa cakes (if they're not) will be displayed on a plate
to look at for the duration. An average session should
last forty-five intense minutes. If you go over you are

placing your host in an invidious position. She may be forced to sense a pending fit or a visit from a plumber to make you leave. Neither excuse is likely to be real.

My first coffee morning went like this. I was obviously nervous. I didn't know the mother well and my mind was on other things; mainly the chaos and failure of my life, and the shopping, naturally. I also knew this mother had two children and was therefore superior to me. She could talk about 'handing down' her older child's clothes – something out of my reach and I knew it. However, I had been invited. I pressed the bell. As the last note faded I was let in via the porch. I tiptoed along the plastic footpath leading to the kitchen. What proof of good parenting, I told myself. Her children obviously went to the park regularly for fresh air and would of course return with muddy boots from such healthy endeavour. No sit 'n' watch video city this. In fact, perhaps I, too, should have a plastic footpath for my hall? Then I started to wonder where I could purchase such an item. I didn't want to ask her where she got hers. She might think I was taking the Mickey; I know I would if it was me. This preoccupied me, so I wasn't concentrating when the social niceties started. The mother said, 'I've got something in the microwave,' at the same time as offering me a coffee. I looked at the whirring microwave and thought, for no good reason, 'Oh no, croissants! Help!' Being on a strict diet at the time, I said, 'Oh no, thank you, I can't.'

She looked hurt and surprised. 'Oh. Water then?'

'Um . . . a . . . a coffee would be lovely, if you have any,' I replied, tentatively.

She looked at me for three seconds. Normal eye contact is just two seconds if you're sitting in a kitchen talking, says Desmond Morris – so I knew things weren't going very smoothly. But she set about switching the kettle back on.

'The kettle's just boiled!' is the traditional greeting at a coffee morning, so I can see how rejecting I must have appeared. I didn't realise how people can speak on two or more topics at once. Social isolation does terrible things to you.

It got worse. When the microwave finally pinged and she moved to its door I leapt off my bar stool and said in a panic, still expecting croissants to emerge, 'No. No, not for me, really!'

I trailed off as I saw a lump of red mincemeat emerge. She was defrosting it for her husband. That's what they eat, after all, I reminded myself. I felt foolish. She ignored the outburst. Why would she be offering me raw mince at a coffee morning anyway? No. We both said nothing. A mug of instant came my way. It was fig rolls, so they were easy to resist. Then the fellowship started to reveal itself.

Of course, hurdles had to be got through before I was let into her confidence. The apparent superior reading standard of her children, the amount of friends she can call upon for the school run, the amount of weekend away-breaks as 'a family' they have done with other 'families', the charming school uniform and extra piano lessons (grade five was mentioned). But then, if you're a good listener and you hide your envy, you will be rewarded. I eventually hit the jackpot.

This woman had been married *five times*! Yes. Five. I warmed to her instantly. I forgave her everything . . . the bloodied meat, the cherried toaster, the reading ability, the children's orchestra debut. Instead, I asked how did she *do* it? How did she recover, how long did it take to get over one? What kind of court case? Did he really try and legally possess her stripped pine dressing-table? Why?

It is amazing. Once you dig deep over that coffee mug you find you are not alone. All right, you'd rather they were suffering at the same time as you, but you can't have everything. The fact that they've been there at all, and survived should be sufficient. We are all equal, even if their surfaces are more gleaming than ours, and their mantlepiece more throbbing with invites than mine. Digging deep can give you solace. This mother, having had three disasters and two children, had devised a successful system of selection for a fifth partner. 'A wall chart,' she said. I was surprised.

She explained. 'You do ticks by the pluses and crosses by the impossibles.' It then made complete sense. She gave me some useful examples. Admittedly, our priorities were at odds, but I got the idea.

Her pluses for husband number five were: can he drive? Tick. Does he like golf? Tick (this would have been a cross for me, but it takes all sorts).

Crosses included: he likes beetroot. A cross but can live with. Not the body of Tom Cruise. A cross: and Tom's deceptively short, anyway.

She concluded that as the man could drive she would go for it. Even if his teeth were permanently pink from the beetroot. It could be worse, she said.

I resolved to start a wall chart of my own. Then I remembered I'd just jettisoned my last partner for guiding me around too much. He was obsessed with steering me into chairs, or moving me about the house for no apparent reason. I lost all control in the end as I waited for him to reposition me. It's funny, it's the little things, isn't it? So I didn't have a person to do my wall chart for. But she gave me a list of things to do in preparation for number two proper. I went home clutching my mantra.

Back home, I lit a candle and unfolded my karma.

1. Go to pubs, wine bars and activity holidays (with her).
2. Always include friends in glamorous foursomes (her plus three of mine).

3. Join a gym with a guest pass facility (for her).
4. Get some Jaffa cakes in (for her).

    (She said she'd come to mine next time.)

It's funny, I had the distinct feeling that she was on the look-out for number six. Perhaps eating beetroot was really a cross, then? Well, if a coffee morning can help chase the blues and make you purposeful, who needs analysis?

On the other hand, I'll tell you about my first coffee morning as host . . .

I made the mistake of asking three mothers at once – to make the house full of atmosphere. I was frightened of just one mother at a time. I'd have to put the dryer on for background noise, but unfortunately it drives me crazy. I start talking very fast so God knows what I'd be like with an unfamiliar mother person at the same time. Then I thought I might put a Pogues tape on, but then they might think it was some sort of Ceilidh dance

class and not a coffee morning at all. If I put Radio 4 on, the discussion would conflict with ours and we might be distracted. No, it definitely had to be Radio 2. A bit like being in the foyer of a motel.

Jaffa cakes, instant coffee and a few bold mugs were all that was needed. I went to a brand-new mothers' tea once, and the mother had baked a cake. We all hated her for it. It was brown, under a plastic cover like an offering on an altar, next to her nappies-to-be-collected. We ate it, mind you. We didn't want to be that rude.

Anyway, they all arrived at the same time. I think they'd ganged up at one of their houses for a pre-coffee-morning coffee which got me paranoid. No sooner had I said the regulation 'Kettle's just boiled!' and switched the radio on, than they all wanted daytime TV. Apparently, there was a sexy shrink on doing eating disorders.

At least I didn't have to worry about the conversation. It always flows when the TV is on. I think it was a success. They all left when the programme finished. When I've found a plastic 'walk-way' for the hall, I'll have another one.

16

COMPROMISE:
A VERY CYNICAL OVERVIEW

Here is a word very much in vogue. Instead of compatability, attraction, or the simple Cor . . . !, now the question on everyone's lips is 'Yes, yes, but can she compromise?'

To have compromise ability if you are female means being able graciously to give in on what colour to paint the walls, where to get the take-away, who drives who home, etc. If you say 'No, after you,' and 'What do you think?' and 'No, *let me* do the washing-up,' a lot, then compromise ability is what you've got. You should flaunt it. Don't bother going to the gym to work out for the perfect body – just say 'I think that's a good idea! Well done,' and all will be well.

This ability, if found in males, can cause fear and loathing from their colleagues. They complain they may 'lose their identity' – in other words be prevented in some way from playing tennis, swimming, drinking, or whatever it is they enjoy. You often see these men in pubs on a Sunday lunchtime up at the bar, rubbing their hands over their buttocks (not each other's – in this group anyway), and laughing knowingly at any 'poor sod' who has got himself one of those 'compromise relationships'. They may toast his hoovering or dusting in a nervous sort of way.

It has to be said, the male compromisers are rare. But they make up for it by marrying the female version, and books have been written to make it all a yarn and a lark and not sinister at all. Cricket widows. Golf widows. Tennis widows, to name but three.

So as long as *one* half of the Compro duo is busy doing it, you're OK. I'm always meeting the 'gratefully and worthily still marrieds' who constantly drop the C word to prove that they are THINKING PEOPLE and NO, IT DOESN'T COME EASY, BUT THEN YOU'VE GOT TO COMPROMISE, HAVEN'T YOU? Great, say I. Have a sandwich.

In my past, 'Let's compromise' often meant a flaky 'No, you can't! But what about this . . . !' One of my first such compromises was when I sacrificed seeing the Monkees live at Wembley to sit through the Royal Tournament, wheezing due to my allergy to horses' excrement. All because a cousin was staying and liked things military. Compromises have always had a bad odour since then.

Now, the word 'compromise' is offered to provide the key and, more importantly, the glue to modern marriages. These 'born agains' spout its virtues like they've just discovered penicillin. These wives will say, 'Well, you've got to work at it, haven't you?' Followed by a nervous laugh that doesn't convince anyone.

On the other hand, one shouldn't be cynical. No. I would be very up for compromise. In fact, I'm dying to try it out. But sometimes being available to compromise on a suck-it-and-see type basis can frighten a man off because then he wouldn't have a good reason for going and – oh gosh – he might have to stay. Not that I'm bitter. Only joking . . .

17

WEDDINGS: OTHER PEOPLE'S

Weddings are inevitable and historically powerful.

We know this empirically because there has never, ever been a wedding-free epoch. Marriages maketh history. And a lot of other bother besides.

In the fourteenth century, medieval banquets marked the coupling of two key offspring to safeguard the land and have a mild ale and lardy cake piss-up to keep the surfs happy and get the rumblings of early capitalism whirring. (I know I wasn't there, but I've been to re-enactments at Hatfield House.) Then, in the sixteenth century, Henry VIII, one of our first serial spouses, had his exes done-in to ensure they didn't turn up and embarrass him and spoil his big day. (If only the facility was extended to commoners.) Who knows what advice could have been proffered from one ex to another? 'Don't do it, he's got a small 'un.' Or even, 'Don't do it, he's got the pox.' Might have been handy for those later afflicted. But would they have listened? I know I didn't.

Even Adam and Eve must have had some kind of reported knees-up in The Bible, even if the numbers were confined to a minimum – before it all went tragically wrong.

Basically, most people want at least one wedding in their lifetime. 'Just to see.' Why should they be diddled out of receiving those once in a lifetime pickings: crystal vases, strange light fittings which need sophisticated electrical assembly work to erect, salad bowls (always), china lattice sweet baskets, all arranged nicely for the rest of the married life, under the stairs.

My mother advised me at the time – final stages of pregnancy – that she thought, on balance, it was probably best to do it than not, which demonstrates her level of faith in the whole thing. 'You can always get divorced later, dear,' she added. The rest is history. At least she had something to write about in her Christmas cards. 'Bought a hat at last.'

A wedding is really a photo opportunity for floral two-pieces with sticky-out hems. Altered for the day because they are usually borrowed. Time stands still for fashion at weddings, luckily.

The function of a wedding is to provide the initiation ceremony after which you are fully entitled to give the following: barbeques; advice to single people, even if they are older than you; 'Open house with Glühwein' for the neighbours at Christmas. The day marks the rite of passage from insecure/single to relieved/coupled. You can safely say that, once married, you can be Prime Minister (if *only* Ted had got himself a wife, we might not have got Maggie; *that's* how important weddings are), head of the Anglican Church or the local Brownies, anything, in fact, where you need to be seen to have legal sex with A.N. Other.

Identifiable legal sex is the mainstay of society. To practise this with permission, in shared accommodation, reassures the world that you are not mad, bad or dangerous to know and can now hold office in all things – even parenthood . . .

I remember all the aunties were at my wedding, buzzing about full of advice such as, 'Don't worry, the worst is over' . . . Funnily enough, they were wrong. It got much worse. But at least it was a chance to get out and meet new people. And it was very exciting. I wore my wedding kit which caused quite a stir. I hadn't been eight months pregnant when I had it fitted so it was a bit . . . tight. If only I'd had the foresight to plan my unplanned pregnancy.

And the thing about being pregnant, particularly on honeymoon if you have one, is that you have to buy bigger clothes and you have to get them all from Mothercare, because they have a monopoly on the dumpy frumpy Shaker look for some reason. Actually, to be fair they are trying to get more trendy but there is something quite demeaning about boogying on down wearing a tartan pinafore dress with a baby rabbit on the pocket. You can go more up-market, of course, and try the sophistocates maternity wear. These shops are usually tucked around the corner from Harrods or Beauchamp Place. In fact, find any cul de sac which is pronounced differently to its spelling and you will normally find a posh shop selling maternity tights and broderie anglaise feeder bras. They are called 'Bébé' or 'Bambino'. Here, all the outsize fluorescent sweaters have sequinned motifs dotted across the chest. They are sometimes difficult to read due to the shadow cast by the enormous shoulder pads. But once you remove these you can easily make out cute yet knowing slogans like, 'It started with a kiss'. I suggested they do another batch with 'It ended with divorce!!' but the shop assistant was Italian and unimpressed with my wry wit and canny sense of reality.

The only other wedding I've been to, apart from mine, was that of a male friend. A friend I'd never snogged nor ever wanted to, ever. However, it soon became necessary to clear my name.

I discovered from several sympathetic cousins and aunties at the reception, that everyone thought I was an 'ex'. Even his mother had been very worried about me due to the child factor and my age, and we'd never even met! I felt a burden before I'd had a pineapple chunk on a cheese and a stick.

To keep numbers down I arrived alone and stood sheepishly; just me and a prawn in a filo sac with no one else's mouth to proprietorially dust the crumbs from.

The remaining singles – without legally recognised spouses – were placed on the one table, to contain and limit the amount of distress caused to other family groups. Non-heterosexuals, thrice-marrieds and other minority groups were left to introduce themselves to each other and hopefully not get too loud.

After a few drinks, whilst still standing I told anyone who'd listen and a few who didn't that, interestingly, I'd never even *snogged* the groom – so keen was I to clear my name. As it turned out, I was telling the bride's sister, the bride's mother and then the bride herself. (I'd never met her, so how could I have known? Everyone who isn't in floral is in white silk nowadays.) One cousin even said to me, 'I was watching your face while he made his speech. You're very brave.' She looked kindly upon me.

'Am I?' I replied in surprise. My expression had been one of 'I wonder when there'll be a break, can I make it to the loo without being noticed, and where the hell is it anyway?'

Given that my sense of pity threshold is quite low, caused by the single parent front, I really didn't need an unwarranted extra dose of pity on my day off, thank you. I was just saying all this to the priest, and how unjust it all was, when I was rewarded at last with comprehension – he nodded excitedly at me. I thought, hello, someone understands. How appropriate it should be from a man of the cloth, perhaps I should convert. But he was nodding excitedly at the French waiter – Priesty was really into the deep-fried mushrooms and spicy dip and he urged me to try 'a bit of heaven' by thrusting me an empty cocktail stick. I couldn't help feeling that this was a deeply symbolic gesture from him to me, and also a metaphor for the day itself. However, I kept my thoughts to myself which was sensible, given I had no-one to talk to.

The difficult thing about being a single parent at such a symbolic event as a wedding is how different generations of the nuclear families who have all met up for it, deal with you. I bumped into one half of a couple who'd been married successfully for thirty affluent years. After a quick 'How's your father? Oh, dead. Sorry. And your husband? Oh, yes sorry . . .' she said nervously. 'Now where *is* that husband of mine?!' Did she think he'd take this opportunity to scarper, having been despatched for vol au vents and a serviette?

The niece also had an awkward moment when her spouse went to the loo. It was worth it for him, though. He got a hero's welcome when he returned, and was practically blow-jobbed for the duration of the speeches.

Anyway, a footnote about the wedding poetry. A blushing bridesmaid full of taffeta and purpose went up to read an extract from one of the W.H. poets – not Auden, he's been done to death – Bates or Smith, I recall. Anyway, she'd edited it so thoroughly she had the congregation thinking that, for some inexplicable reason, she'd gone up to examine the vicar's plinth, exhale loudly and then return, flushed, to her pew. Weddings – who'd have them?

18

ORGANISATION, IT'S A JUGGLE

There once was a book called *Superwoman*
Which made a lot of dosh
But now the lady author says
Did I write *that*? Oh gosh!

Like all those people who foolishly say they're not for turning – they always do. In the end. You can't make a stand *and* make a fortune from making a stand (Shirley, Rosemary, Germaine, Margaret) and expect those views to remain in vogue. So, you either retire to your well-earned chateau or you make capitulation marketable and write another book Mark 2. As Carly says, 'Nothing stays the same,' which is something I hang on to after a bad day.

Juggling takes a lot of energy, as those of us who read *She* magazine will know. A more passive approach might appeal. You can practise this from the comfort of your own armchair. You just have to repeat acceptingly, 'Life's organic, it's a process.' This was told to me by a herbalist in a headscarf whom I consulted while getting myself off hard drugs. Aspirins and Night Nurse weren't really *solving* anything.

So, as I sipped my foul-tasting herbal stress remedy I had to really believe that life was a process. 'It's bound to throw up something new once the leaves have infused,' I said to myself, almost convincingly. Not too

many guarantees on this one, unfortunately, and I soon realised I had to get out there, get active, and take advice from a how to book.

Superwoman, by Shirley Conran, became my guide. Although not entirely appropriate for my non-executive and carefree lifestyle, the handy hints stuck in my mind for their optimism. She really believed at the time of writing that it was possible to: live in a perfect home, have a permanently pristine car inside and out, be on top of the shopping, be the best in the workplace and have the sexual appetite (fulfilled, of course) that one had before pair bonding and nappies – before, in fact, life had taken over . . . A very optimistic view indeed.

Detail is all in this book. Shirley advises, for instance, that by having a selection of art postcards (Musée d'Orsay, not Gordon and Fraser) in your top drawer, *already stamped*, the reader is then deemed equipped for most anything. I gaffawed at this at first. But then

I saw the light. It does help your sense of efficiency and control. I felt so efficient one day when I calmly put my hand in my drawer and re-selected an already selected and stamped card, ready to send off to someone I owed money to such as United Dairies. She was right! I was able to connect into the social grid instantly and I didn't even have to delay matters by driving to the post office to get a stamp. The delay was more leaving it on the table for two weeks before remembering to post it.

The tips are endless, but the car chapter is worth a mention here. The suggestion of having a bin-liner concealed in your glove compartment to collect rubbish, as well as a special Hoover 'Petite' for the nooks and crannies, blew my mind. Surprisingly, auto cranny hygiene is a priority. Used Opal Fruits, leaking Ribena cartons and old balloons which won't burst do not give a sense of control and are collectively strangely depressing. So, thank you, Shirley.

Why not try for a pain-free, easy-does-it, single-parenting lifestyle, especially devised for 'Today's woman who juggles'? We don't want to be left behind, and we must be organised in the face of the gleaming, rubbish-free Range Rover convoys on the school run, Hoover 'Petite' ostentatiously displayed on the back seat. (Complacent cows.) Not that I've got a chip. It's their problem. Allow me to modestly add some more tips along these lines. Right. Get a pen and note down this crucial list in your note-pad with attached biro conveniently stuck to the inside of your pint-sized Filofax. (Like Shirley would have.)

1. **Headed note paper** is all. You will need this for the impressive novels you send to your solicitor.
2. **Word processor**. This rules out any personal presentation throughout communication with the ex. Handwriting recognition can cause nostalgia and rage, or indeed nostalgia for rages past, depending on how far down the line you are.
3. **A fax machine**. Or, if you're skint, select one from a skip and tune it up. There are loads of jettisoned circa '89 PCs in Clapham and Holland Park just because they're not the right colour any more. Now you can communicate painlessly, impersonally and in silence to the other side re: access or other necessaries. No sucking in of teeth, no barely disguised hysteria, no incitement to verbal violence – nothing ugly need take place. Instead, an efficient emotion-free missive of *pure* info. (Fax machines don't pick up cerebral tremors, thankfully.)
4. **Stamps**. Make that annual drive to the post office and stock up on one hundred weight of stamps. So, you have word processor, you have fax, and you have stamps, if, God forbid, your fax paper runs out. Now you are part of a communication system *on your terms*.

PS: the arty cards can be used to say thank you to other mothers for the 'lovely tea' and, 'Sorry about the broken goldfish bowl, hope the enclosed will make up for it. (He should survive postage time – I checked with the pet shop. They advised perforated Jiffy bags. Hope our hole-puncher wasn't too big for him). You have to be accommodating, especially if you don't possess the husband to bring out once a year. But don't try too hard. That's counter-productive – you might get a reputation for being desperate.

It must be pointed out, though, there are occasions when one's sense of organisation can become excessive. I know a mother who is so entrenched in the organising thing that, whether she be sunning herself on the beach, having a foot massage, or even participating in plain interactional sex, she always says the same thing: 'How are we doing for time?' Everyone obediently dives for their watches – and the moment is lost.

But finally, let us not forget you can also fight the opposition in your garden. The fully equipped garden will stand you in good stead in the face of all nuclear deterrents. You give a good barbie – you get respect. I'm sure Shirley would approve of this technique. First, borrow some money, then phone big Peter Jones and get them to bike over (you'll be too busy pricking the tomato and tarragon sausages to collect) a GARDEN ROCKY ROLLER SWING THING to take up the length, breadth and, in my case, total circumference of your garden. The sight of this serious piece of garden equipment will ensure no-one will mess with you from there on in. It says, 'I'm in control, I'm organised and I have a rocky garden roller.' Enough said, I think.

19

MARKETING SKILLS

If products are labelled well, we all know we'll buy them. They need to be promoted with a push, a patina, a projected image. For example, without advertising we'd never call a plimsoll a 'loafer' or a sandal a 'mule'. But we do. We just say, 'I've got a lovely pair of loafers,' unquestioningly. We don't realise we're part of the big sell. Advertising, hypnotising, propaganda-ising – whatever you call it – has the power to enhance.

No such service for the single parent. I can only presume this is because Big Brother doesn't want to package us. He'd rather take his pick from sweeping us under the carpet or scape-goating, whichever helps balance his books the most.

I am still waiting for the first true-life coffee ad saga.

A female single parent opens her penthouse door. We see a male single parent standing on the doorstep looking sheepish. They exchange smouldering looks, she is holding a jar of coffee. Another telling look, a raised eyebrow, suddenly the son emerges from behind his dad, grabs her jar of coffee and runs inside. A crash, he bumps into her child, spilling the coffee beans all around. Pause for effect. They all laugh knowingly and hug in a coffee-style embrace . . .

Not yet a while. Which is strange, because I drink the stuff all the time.

Just in case some far-reaching advertising executive

is reading this, single parenting is a thing of the past. From now on, it's PERSON SOLO, FEMME INDIVIDUALISTE or even SIGNORA AWARE. Or not. Marketing is all. We all want to be presented as the best, the most honest, the most kind, the most caring person. So, when a couple separates, there is a marketing problem to be sorted. If there are two of you, each will try to come out of it the best. But how does each party sell itself?

Who said 'I'm going'?

Who said 'Good'?

Who said 'Don't go'?

Who said 'Let's try'?

Who said 'We can't'?

And, frankly, who cares? Apart from you and your child?

The sad truth is *no-one*. You'll find, just like cottage cheese, domestic conflict has a decidedly limited shelf-life. Once the news is a few weeks old it becomes non-viable.

Of course, there is that initial response which, like a first kiss, gets dynamic feedback. It will be met with an incredulous 'No! Tell me more!' Your will hear the listener reaching for a chair and dispatching her children to the fridge so she can hear the whole story uninterrupted. No matter that they eat all the ice cream in the freezer, she has set her cap at someone else's misfortunes and is growing in self-confidence by the second. She may even offer 'Do you want to stay here tonight? You can. Look, where are you? I'll come and get you. No, I haven't got a babysitter, we'll all come. No worries. I'll dig us out of the snow, we've got a snow plough anyway, or we can sledge across. You can tell me again when I'm over there. Get the whisky out.'

The same friend, the same problem a few months on, and you get the answering machine.

And so to the official view.

HOW TO TELL THE CHILD, OR WHY YOU LIVE APART BUT ARE BOTH EQUALLY PERFECT IN EVERY WAY

What he may think is the 'truth' or the 'best story' or the 'best truthful story' to explain to the child why he's living it up – whoops – I mean living apart from you is inevitably going to differ from yours.

A good idea is to write a cover version of the history and send it to departed partner to agree with. You may then get accused of re-writing the facts to suit yourself. But how can one get away from that, with the best will in the world, and mine is one of the best, of course? On the other hand, he might thank you for your time but wish to furnish the child with his own truth, thank you very much for interfering. Well, at least you tried to promote and market a secure, well-balanced backdrop for the child's world, even if no-one else will.

Partners may well use videos and books to promote their corner. *Mrs Doubtfire* is a good video from the man's point of view, and is often played to babies to see if they can understand how to apportion blame wisely. If, indeed, there is a question of blame – but that's for the over twos.

If you've got your story straight, you can convince anyone that what is occurring is, on balance, the best system. Hold your ground. Defy any other populist view. Ignore nannies who tell you tales from teatime. 'Oh, it broke my heart . . .' I don't believe this. Nanny is looking very robust and unbroken.

'Little Laura asked where her *daddy* was.' The word DADDY is very dramatically mouthed at me so my child busily lip-reads. 'It was so *sad*.' Another mime. Quite badly done.

'What did she say?' I asked.

'She said he used to live with her but that he doesn't any more, and he sees her a lot,' her mouth pursed down dramatically.

'What's sad about that?' I say. 'It's true.'

'Yes, but you know what I mean.' I do, and I don't like it.

I can feel the familiar paranoia rising. Did the other mother ask the child to ask my child about absent father, and why does Nanny have to have her heart broken by it? Surely she's got other things to worry about, like the meaning of life, for instance. I don't say this. 'Would it have been better to say he ran off to join a circus, perhaps?'

Nanny falters. Unsure for a moment.

'I mean that's what our Prime Minister's father did.' Nanny says 'Mmm . . . ,' still unsure.

This is best. Keep the conversation consistently illogical. With any luck she'll never catch up.

20

TRAVELLING LIGHT (WITHOUT A WEDDING RING)

Imagine the scene. You are slaloming your way through an Intercity train corridor in search of a suitable seat for you and child. The child is attached to a finger, your bags are hung décolleté and otherwise around your person. By bags, I mean stretching-as-it-bumps-along thin plastic bag stuffed with last-minute drawing material, used-up sketch pad and a leaky biro found in station bar, and seductively bright tote bag (present from an optimistic in-law at the birth of child) containing toxic waste, nappies (if necessary), wet-wipes (always necessary), juice, liquid drugs, the biscuit bag (a recycled freezer bag and very sticky) to prevent eating from the sweets bag, and the sweets bag (a crinkled brown paper one) to provide solace when the biscuit bag has been rejected. Right, so, having found a seat (unpeopled with perverts, drug abusers or squaddies as far as the eye can tell under pressure) you unfold yourself, relinquishing bags and child.

All is calm until you see another passenger purposefully heading for your seat. With dismay you see why. Her rightful claim of ownership is displayed on the rack above. One tartan holdall. You can't argue with that. But wait, all is not lost. She is a rosy-cheeked OLD PERSON. She might be persuaded, out of a fondness for young flesh in pigtails, Start-rite shoes and an overdeveloped interest in *Take the High Road*, to activate her concern for family values and compromise her carefully claimed seat by sitting 'facing away' on the empty single opposite. Once settled and feeling no doubt saintly, what harm could she do to your territory? As long as she observes the correct demarcation of space, clearly marked by the Formica table.

Fraternisation while travelling with a child is inevitable, but any further assault on boundaries can be kept at bay as long as the enemy respects occupied territory (the bags, the child and me). As it turned out, it didn't take longer than an accosting 'Oh, deary me' addressed invitingly at us both as she sank into her seat, to find out that Old Person was returning to her home in Dorset having visited happy and loving relatives up in town. This family membership equipped Old Person with total knowledge of children's behaviour and their

needs, a deep-rooted, thematic obsession with all weather conditions (past and present), as well as a keen interest in knitting anything from matinée jackets to loose cardigans. She positively hugged herself with glee at the prospect of travelling home with a child to wink and coo at, with the odd knowing nod at me thrown in.

Would that this status quo could have lasted. I could have coped with that. A bit of real-life Emmerdale Farm. Bigots and rural communities – always a fascinating combination. But all assumptions must be brought to heel as ugly reality steps in. A cruel reminder that really, truly, *you are alone* (except for the bags and the child). Remember, this is not Italy where bambinos will be bambinos. This is Little England, where everything must be composed of neat units with symmetry and order. To be honest, I knew the cover would be blown pretty soon, and it was. We'd been travelling in this sealed social capsule for what seemed like an age when I decided to do a name check on a station – just to get an idea of the amount of social grimacing time still to be covered before we reached our destination. Paddington. Yup. It's true. Time flashes by when you're having fun. And not when you're not. Just as we passed through the first tunnel of many, the child piped up, 'Daddy's got one of those.' (Old Person's tartan holdall.)

I say quickly, 'He *has*, hasn't he!'

Child replies, 'How would you know he's got one?'

I say, 'Well . . . I just do.'

'But how do you *know* he's got one?'

Old Cosy opposite stops her cooing and the knowing nod freezes on her face. She clocks the wedding ring omission. Rustles her *Family Circle* out from her foldaway rain hat cum travel sac.

Child persists, 'If you got married and Daddy got married I'd have two mummies and two daddies!'

'Mmmm,' I affirm as subtly as I can, going direct for

sweet bag by-passing biscuit bag since I have called an internal state of emergency. But no. I'm not quick enough.

Child continues, 'In fact, I'd rather have two mummies because then I might get a mummy who plays with me as well.' The sweet search is arrested.

'What do you mean?' I say, indignant, forgetting Mrs Dorset for a moment. She's busy with her galoshes/slip-ons anyway. 'I play with you.'

'Not much, though.'

I'm not having this. 'What about all the plays? And the dressing-up?' No response, but pensive. 'All right,' I see a chink, 'the Junior Post Office. I'm *always* the customer and you know that.'

Having engaged in battle successfully, child is ready to concede some ground, but not before Mrs Rural Harmony tuts and sloshes off in her galoshing slip-ons towards the tea bar. While we are alone I get stuck in. I hugely resent the implication that I don't play as much as another potential mummy, especially as I'd do anything to get a crack at being the post mistress and I never am. I just have to look at the driving licences and dog discs as my child does all the issuing and stamping. We have finally agreed that it's 50/50 when Oldie turns up with a piece of British Rail fruit cake for child. (She's not managed to glean that they prefer crisps, I notice.)

'Here,' she says, 'have this, poor little mite.' She looks with pity at the illegitimate under five in front of her.

Child hates fruit cake, and tells Farty so. I am pleased. Just for the record, I tell Bigot the child is not illegitimate, but offer the info that I am divorced. Why I do this is beyond me, but the weak become very strong in the face of boundary moving and can induce panic with us boundary movers with one disapproving look. Pathetic, I know. But I have my limits when travelling, the bags and child can diminish my sense of autonomy and power.

'And we wonder why burglary has gone up!' she exclaims.

I wonder, too, but can't see the connection. Then I do. The child has been researching *Family Circle* for useful pages to pull out and tear up for a collage. 'For when we have some glue,' she explains to British National Party Lady.

Luckily, I've spotted some vacant space further down the corridor. The automatic doors will be particularly stimulating if we can just claim the floor space in front of the toilets. In fact I can't think why we bothered with seats in the first place.

21

HOLIDAY PLANNING

The trick in getting older and maturing sensibly – by that I mean avoiding a panic foray into collagen injections and its attendant disappointments – is to LOWER YOUR EXPECTATIONS about life.

Now, being in any kind of even vaguely vulnerable and visible catchment group – furry upper lip, fat squashy fingers, white marbled thighs and bow legs, etc. – makes you very prone to over-reacting and panicking. Equally vulnerable, then, is the single parent planning a holiday.

From the outset, a single-parent holiday has to be *perfect*. It has to provide stability whilst travelling, symmetry of spatial relationships in holiday villa party, surrogate family vibes and virtues, sun, sea and laughter. If you fail on any of these, it will be a disaster and entirely your responsibility. Not true, but an easy trap to fall into.

As the summer months loom, one's head will be spinning with thoughts of other, perfect family units, gleefully looking forward to their fun-filled holidays, either in a caravan (me and one child in a camper van? NO), or the villa of their dreams in Provence. This costa des francs, so you'll need another perfect family to join you to justify expense and also to swell the numbers for instant holiday atmosphere. Eating for one and a half in a French farmhouse overlooking a vineyard seems a bit excessive, not to say silly.

So, planning ahead has to be done in order *not* to fall by the wayside as you wave an insincere *bon voyage* to other family holiday-makers setting off with their xenophobic GB stickers. Have a care, though. May I say here that there is nothing nicer than returning to school in September and hearing about the odd disaster of how a family may have suffered in August. Yes, August *can* still be a wicked month for some. Perhaps all the children got ill on the first day and had to be rushed home, or they got mugged in the duty free, or perhaps the hotel wasn't built or there was a VD scare in the self-catering. Or, best of all, the other family turned out to be a nightmare and the fathers came to fisticuffs on the last night and the holiday medical insurance didn't cover inter-villa violence. Great. Always live in hope for this September song.

However, good, realistic planning is best. Don't do what I did and save my pennies for an exclusive-style brochure the like of which I'd never dare send off for before. Don't madly invite a whole disparate lot of people you don't know very well (with children) to share the villa of your dreams with. You may hope that your child will get an impression of perfection abroad for two weeks, and when they are forty they will look back on this man-made heaven and weep nostalgic tears over a perfect and ecstatic childhood holiday. But, quite honestly, dream on.

Changed behaviour, once incarcerated in someone else's villa, does occur. For no other reason, perhaps, than because, as Forrest Gump reminds us, 'Shit happens.' People take advantage – you might not have noticed that back home in England, because you're not there to watch them avoid washing-up, or count up the number of times anyone in the family group has 'contributed' to the kitty, or even the suggestions box (some villas do have these).

Unless you have masochistic tendencies, which may have contributed to the wrong choice of partner in the first place, don't do it again. Break free of the shackles of scroungers – emotional or fiscal. Just because they are a 'family' does not mean they will necessarily behave well. Expediently, they will forget their eurocheque cards/traveller's cheques/any cash at all when it comes to paying-up time. They make themselves popular with the children by suggesting ice creams all round, but then disappear to buy postcards or a designer suit. They will be out sketching on a ravine when it's time to do the supermarché shop (no loo paper is a good indicator of when one should do this), or they might indulge in gyppy tummy if it's their turn to cook. You can see the true colours of moody family friends when in Sienna in the rain. Married grown-ups will whine at the weather and leave you to 'redcoat' the kids. No playground in sight and bloated tummies from Italian ice lollies – all varieties – you will be forced into stranger and stranger time-fillers. 'How about we all make out we're Space Invaders, right? And hide in the cathedral over there till it stops thundering and then we might hop upside down into the museum and play schools? Eh? You can all be the teachers.' Other parents may well leave you with them, and say benevolently, 'No *you* all go. We'll take the Fiat back and meet you at supper time. You'd like a chance to try the Italian trains, wouldn't you?'

My villa was described as 'The villa to die for'. And, funnily enough, we nearly did. It was not secluded, as they had described. It was looked after by a couple who were very cross that they were not in it instead of us and who liked to 'drop by' once an hour to make sure we were enjoying our holiday to the hilt given it couldn't be them. Had we gone to their brother's restaurant yet? Had we used their cousin's taxi for a tour of Sienna, and how dare we consider using the central heating to combat the chill of a fluke rainy period lasting precisely the duration of our holiday without telling them first. That would be extra. Naturally.

People came and went, changing the atmosphere as the holiday progressed from bad to worse. (My fault. I got cocky. I mean, how often can one announce that one has a villa in Tuscany for the summer? I milked that one at the school gates and got punished accordingly.) In the end, I invited my own mother out. This was a primal death wish I feel, looking back. But I wanted to demonstrate success, achievement, harmony, self-sufficiency and complete non-nuclear independence to her. Not much really. (Remember how the older generation can make us boundary movers a touch insecure.)

So, on the last day I took control. I packed up everything. I drove up with child to open the gates of the mountain drive, so when we left for the airport everything would run smoothly. For some reason I thought driving down the mountain road with my packed car and mother inside and *then* opening the gates would appear inefficient. I wanted the gates to be open *first*. I wanted it all done effortlessly and painlessly. Well, my child and I duly drove up the road to open the gate, having left the mother inside the villa to have a relaxing final cappuccino. Then, for some reason, I rolled the car down the mountain drive for fun. *Don't* ask me why. Because I was single and stressed? If there had been another bod in car they may possibly have explained that you don't roll cars down steep gradients because the steering will lock and you won't be able to break on a hire-car Fiat Uno because they don't come with effective breaks for tourists.

My last words were, 'Oh, no!' which is an enigmatic epitaph, or perhaps not. I'm exaggerating. Obligingly, the car did eventually decide to stop, but only when we were half-on and half-off the mountain and hanging from a precipice. We clambered out and returned to the blissfully unaware mother. We revealed to her that, thankfully, we were still alive, and best not go down the mountain drive to look at our hire-car hanging off the mountain-side. She did anyway.

We were eventually rescued from our remote villa by the cousin of the solicitous couple. They knew someone who had a fork-lift truck and who dropped us off at the airport where, needless to say, we missed our plane.

But was it worth it? The panic about trying to be perfect and smooth-running and in control can be too much. The next year I stayed in during August. Got the garden hose out. Got browner then before with no pressure of sightseeing or childwatching in the pool. Inflatables are just as wet but with no deep end.

THE GREAT ARE OUTDOORS

HOLY DAYS are, historically, religious festivals where you can stop doing what you normally do and get holy – namely pork out at Christmas, fatten up at Easter, or get gutted on vats of lager in August. The Pope may not have ordained the August one, but he did set the trend for time off. Even Prince Charles has to slip his seasonal fishing in. (Each to his own ground sheet – as long as he does no harm to the fish and doesn't give the river a bad name.)

And I, too, can see that the great outdoors has a lot to offer. I am reminded of this as I raise my face to catch the speckles of rain in the morn, as I step on to the mat to collect the milk, when I walk the two paces to the car, and then again when I've driven round the corner and got out of the car and stepped into the newsagent. The ritual morning grunt reminds me how nice it would be to get a 'Hello' one day, or even 'Thanks for shopping here! We love you!' I take the dream further, and imagine a holiday where I could feel those same speckles of rain for more than ten seconds a throw. (The Lake District always has special offers with that in mind.)

But once you've tasted a freedom like this you might start to want more. You might start thinking about the chance of some sun in between those clouds, and what about a swim? It's all there for the asking. And ask you must, no-one's going to *offer* you anything. Free. Without conditions, that is. I can remember the days when one had the inclination to have a voyeuristic laugh over the Lonely Hearts section in *Time Out*, and then, for decency's sake, peruse the travel section to see the same thing offered but under the less socially desperate heading of 'Wanted, Travel Companion' instead of 'A last ditch attempt at fraternisation – any kind – from a desperate guy in deep denial' on the earlier pages. All you had to do – the ad implied – was head out to Australasia or Brussels with the invariably inadequate guy. And, for your free ticket, let them do it to you – fraternise – in a tent, Volkswagen or the QE2, depending on the size of his budget. I suggest you avoid this if you can.

There are other ways to go on a non-nuclear holiday, and you can enjoy it as a single P. One way is by teaming up with friends. If you have any suitable. I managed to scrape together one single-parent friend upon becoming single, which was a one hundred per cent mark-up from before. It was all quite casual; I just rang the friend up on the off-chance (it took three weeks to find her in) and then sobbed and begged her for help, sharing my plight with her as pointedly as I dared through the tears. You must be precise about what you want, or you might be sent a food parcel or old baby clothes. Remember not to lose sight of your goal. *You* want a holiday, and someone told you that *she's* got a flat in Greece. Once you've established that this isn't just a malicious rumour to raise your hopes and make a fool out of you, or worse, she's sold the darn thing, get cracking on the deal.

Why would she help you? Because people feel guilty, at certain times in their lifecycles. I have noticed that Sorted Out People can become distraught with guilt about being so Sorted Out, and unless people like me seek them out, they feel obliged to go and work in a 'Change-of-A-Dress' shop and start being snotty to the customers because really they are rather cold in this unheated temporary premises and secretly despise the murky clothing. So, in that way, I'm relieved to conclude that the equation balances. Give and take. I help her not work in a charity shop, and she helps me with everything else.

I took a risk on this particular choice of potential holiday provider as I had not had any contact with her for most of my adult life. She must have had a very short memory because, regrettably, I did do her harm. When we were younger, a short while back, we were anticipating a rather promising disco in Catford. Promising meaning that boys would be there. I did her make-up for her, completely covering her eyelids in black Flo-master. Abi Opharim was very big at the time, I told her she was the spit. Surprisingly, she believed me. I justified this sabotage with the fact that she was better-looking than me, and could take a knock-back. The next day her mother rang up my mother and demanded that she pay the optician's bill. Indelible ink and contact lenses were not chemically friendly, and there wasn't a wilful abuse clause on her insurance. Fair enough, I thought. The mother didn't.

Back to the call. If one is too grateful to the potential holiday contact it may give her ideas. She may end up feeling so benevolent that she can afford to become selfish. Before I knew it, the ten days in her holiday flatlet started to lead ominously to a part-exchange deal of babysitting, cooking and entertaining her emotionally charged children. She was reminded of how she'd had enough of her kids, and recalled how there was that Greek barman who gave her one in the early 80s, and perhaps with a child-free evening she might invite him to replenish her orb? Pardon? That's what he had called it, her orb, that moonlit night down on the beach. But, of course, that was before she had given birth. Before long, my friend was insisting I come for the full two weeks. In fact, she was begging me.

I asked for further details. Crete. That's across the sea then, because we know England and Wales. And the ticket? Couldn't we pay more? I mean, will we get up in the *air* for that price? Where will we all sleep? Top 'n' tail? Well, at least it's Greek soil! Tiles. And it's where? Above a pub on the beach. Great. At least the children won't sleep then . . . WAIT, what am I saying? By which time it was too late.

We met at Stanstead. We splashed out on a train to get there. We saved so much on the plane we went first class. This train journey, with the full monty of British Rail crusty rolls and executive breakfast Beaujolais, turned out to be the best part of the holiday. I discovered two things. One, it's difficult with other people's children who aren't too happy about their mum's orb being revisited and, two, I hate rabbits. (In moussaka. Dead.)

Another way to holiday is to ditch the companion idea and simply go solo with an absolutely reduced away-day ticket. EuroDisney is a real favourite. Now that's EuroDisney in France, not to be confused with Disney World in the States. Indeed, it never will be. EuroDisney in France is the high-street version, for the plebs. It's brilliant. Less than a tenner will get you to a huge play park area in the middle of nowhere just outside Paris. It's nearer than Florida and you don't need a bulletproof Babygro to get there, so why not?

Once you slip through the gates you've got one hour to enjoy yourself. Take away five hours queuing time and you've already missed your plane back before you've arrived. It's the only way they can force people to stay in the EuroDisney hotels. Before which you have to brave possibly the scariest of rides. The hotel connecting bus. Which doesn't. It inches forward as you fend off Piglet or Tigger as they come on board to shake you by the paw. Which is the closest I've got to smelly acrylic since my granny's loose covers caught fire.

And, obviously, it rains there. Where else would you site it except a large, uncovered open space if you sold regulation Mickey Mouse rainproof ponchos? I felt I really belonged after completing the first two-hour queue for my yellow poncho. Soon I was like everyone else. Desperate, wet, powerless and hungry. I eventually found a burger bar, two hours later, but I knew it was the right place because it had the longest queue and I'd spotted a lot of other desperate divorced parents doing quality time in it. Three more hours of queuing with them and we were finally able to open our Eurofood cartons. Only to find the gravest omission of all time – no chips. I was on my knees now, as you can imagine. Please, I sobbed. Please don't make me queue again for chips. I beg you. I'll do anything, anything, just name it. Name what you want. She said she wanted to go home. Immediately. I said it's a deal.

This experience of being out of control abroad brought me back to the camper van idea. Perhaps I had been hasty in my dismissal of the delights of DIY in the UK . . . And I discovered that going on a camper van weekend can be unusual. You won't need longer than a weekend to discover this.

As a single parent you might have to wait till a married friend (the one with the camper van) has split up from their partner, so there's space in the front seat. It's usually men who invest in these vans in the first place. They do that out of guilt – for not seeing the children enough – then they bugger off before using it. The first wave of guilt is the most lucrative. (For those left behind.) Use it.

You will drive off to the New Forest and erect an enormous dome of canvas under which you will all bed down. (A bit like tepee meets Dun Roamin' in style.) The showers, complete with used verruca plasters as well as pin-ball machines are all within hopping-over-tent-pegs-in-the-mud distance, and all you do is pour yourself a few beers and talk about when you last had sex. This may not take long, but at least you can rest in the knowledge that the children will be communing with nature. Nuts

(dry roasted) and berries (hopefully not poisonous, but
you can't be everywhere to check after five lagers) will
keep them content until it's time for their chips at the
Gang Land Camper Van Convention Hut for under fives.
Nice.

22

HALF TERM

Let's do the break away
Let's do the fake away
Let's do the make-the-time-up celebration

When all gets dark and lost and confounding and you
don't get to see your young person for enough time
because you are earning the crust even though she's
the one who likes you best out of everybody, and you
only get to see the people who like you about twentieth
best on average most of the time – which seems entirely
illogical but necessary – you might wake up one morning
and come to your senses. It's your child's very first half
term and *you've got to do something*.

... PARTICULARLY ALARMING WHEN YOU REALISE YOU HAVEN'T EVEN BEEN ASKED TO TEA WITH ANYONE

There was nothing in the diary at all. Actually, we
didn't have one but if we did it would have been empty.
I wasn't put off. I propped a notebook by the phone to act
as our social calendar-to-be, and decided to infiltrate the
tea-party network. If the sandwiches wouldn't come to
me, I would dial someone's mother and make my own.
    The first call is the easiest. Anyone can say 'We're

desperate to have Clare round to tea.' It's best to make
the stakes high. But can you really hack it? Suddenly,
'tea' can take on a gastronomic weight. Given that
you've had the audacity to invite another four-year-old
to sample your wares, you've got to make sure you do
it right. I thought of appropriate reference points. Enid
Blyton would most likely turn to Harrods or Fortnums
for her spread. I reminded myself of *The Secret Seven*.
They were *always* having tea. In fact, problem solving
for them revolved around teas, which must have made
them all quite tubby if you think about it. One would
need the correct kind of sponge roly poly, and angel cake
and a three-tiered sponge with frosty icing. I wondered
if the talking Yellow Pages offered a frosting service to
save time? But animal biscuits would do for starters,
wouldn't they? To hell with E numbers and manic behaviour, they look tea-timish.

Once I got Clare's mum on the phone, I launched into
Mother mode. Jolly yet business-like. No soul, mind.
Never talk about being depressed or having thrush to
a mother you've never met whose child you need to
network with. This is very wrong. I set about securing a
'mutually convenient time' followed by Knowing Laugh.
Always have a few dates up your sleeve. That way you
disarm the other mother by demonstrating your own
importance, and delight her by making a window for her
despite your own commitments. I sped things along by
offering an 'Oh, it's so complicated, isn't it!' deceitfully
glancing at my own empty notebook-cum-calendar-to-
be. The other mother then duly claimed her rightful
opportunity to reveal her rich and varied timetable for
the next quarter. For good measure, she itemised the
events they had to sadly turn *down*. This narration of
Jennifer's diary (she was called Jennifer) finally came
to a close and we purred together knowing she was
satisfied that, through the audio narration of events,

we had bonded as like-minded parents, honest and true. Little did she know. So finally, to a rather nauseating fanfare provided by myself, (I said 'Hurrah!') a window was decreed suitable for the tea to take place. We both heaved a sigh of relief. Hers regretful – she clearly enjoyed this kind of caper – mine genuine.

But, of course, it had to be *after half term*. '*Of course!*' I echoed. It was beginning to feel like that scene in *Fatal Attraction* when Glenn Close keeps popping back up in the bath, just when you think it's all over. Then it all started to go wrong. I, over-confident with my placement in the mother's tea catchment nexus, got cocky and ventured into discussing further the merits of half term. I said, 'Thank goodness for half term!' I said this because it's a change from non-half term and it goes down well if you affirm change. It's so *windy*, it's so rainy, it's so hot – all are acceptable meeting points on the short-term-exchange mother's think tank. However, this mother then said, 'Yup. We've got a time-share in the Pyrenees. Thank God.' Thank God indeed.

But this addenda to the business in hand was my undoing. I said 'The Pyrenees – how lovely!' Then I added, foolishly, 'Whereabouts in the Pyrenees?' Why I needed to know this minor detail I can't imagine. Never, never challenge their hold on things. They have just told you they have a time-share in the Pyrenees. Why did I have to take it further? There was a silence and I knew all was not well. An embarrassed silence wherein prior control was surrendered. She didn't know! Oh God! I'd inadvertently caught her out. Either it's a lie and they're not really going or, worse, they are going but she doesn't know where they are going exactly and I've made her look like she's lying even though she isn't! I stupidly perservered with my mistake. 'Because I know the Pyrenees . . .' NO. NON. NEIN. NIET. Never pull rank. She's the one with the time-share in the bloody place. You haven't even got a shed there. Don't mess. She's got the Volvo, the several children, the husband, and now the time-share in the Pyrenees. *You* are the one without the husband and only the one child, and how dare you know about the Pyrenees. I said – to fill her flustered silence – 'Well, anyway, how lovely to get away . . . tea would be great on the 7th . . .' tail off. Cringe. All that ground lost! I should have said 'All right for some!' It's the paradoxical stalwart used by all mothers as they roar off in their Jeeps to somewhere else important.

Anyway, given it was still half term and my tea network connection, although successful, had been pushed back to the post half-term period, it got me thinking. If I was going to do something tangible with the time, I'd better have a mini break. And you can't get minier than the Isle of Wight. It's not very far, but far enough to feel far away. We would cross water on a boat together, stay in a B and B together, and do children's things non-stop together until the half-term sentence was up. I blanked out my EuroDisney experience (see Chapter 21) where queuing for a ride on a teacup in the rain had done me in. No. This was to be a more dignified away break for me and child.

The quite interesting thing about providing one-to-one attention with a child when *you* have the time, is that it won't coincide with a time when the child wants it. Or, worse, they might want the attention but take this opportunity to punish you for not giving them the attention before when they wanted it more. A complacent rudeness will pervade because you are in public and they know they've got you over a barrel. I find my voice taking on a falsely calm and even tone of inventive rationalisation.

You do wonder what it's all for at times, particularly when you catch your child playing ecstatically with a friend and laughing deliriously at a cardboard box. Why did you bother with butterfly houses, zoos, wax museums, doll shops, two theme parks, not to mention risking your life on an exposed toboggan ride, with an audience.

Because there are just the two of you, defences wear thin very quickly. Panic buying sets in fast. My panic purchase on the Isle of Wight was a talking parrot with new batteries. This was switched on in the breakfast room of the B and B. The parrot imitated all sounds within an extensive radius. Including the tight-lipped Virginia Bottomley lookalike on my left, who'd been having a right old go at our best-loved royals from behind her morning *Telegraph*. She concluded waspishly that some of them were just upstarts with no respect.

The parrot obligingly repeated this news for all and sundry in decibels Alexander Bell would have been thrilled with. Miss Uptight glared at me. Everyone else looked distressed at the intrusion. We scooped up our crayons, taking the paper napkins out of the marmalade, and left to get the earlier ferry.

Once a mother is alone with her child and confined to a dining room, older women without children will take it upon themselves to see how many pleases and thank-yous your child can muster before writing you off as an appalling single parent. If a father, however, sat in the same dining room with the same child on a half-term away break, Uptight Lady would, I'm sure, have found the parrot quite quaint, and launched into an indulgent story about how when she was a little girl she, too, had just such a parrot, etc. The whole dining room would whisper behind their kedgeree just *how* that *poor* father came to be alone with that *adorable* child. The story would be coaxed out of the father and he would glory and swell in all this admiration and praise.

Our return from the mini break was met with great news. Jennifer had rattled her diary again and come up with an offer! Apparently there'd been a cancellation. What joy! A child's mother had let them down at the last minute (she wasn't named out of decency, but you got the impression she was something nasty on the bottom of a shoe), and there was now a space in the tea scheduling for us that very day!

So off we went. I was told to return at six to collect. The posher you are, I discovered, the less attention to food you need make. I resolved to jettison my plans for a four-tiered jelly-bean theme cake. No scrummy scones and sugar fancies here. No. Sensible fish stew with lentil sauce. And an orange for pudding. Yup. That was it. Or was she lying to me? I'll never know.

I'll offer them lentils or Swiss roll. That way I'm covered. Three guesses for which one they choose.

23

SEX AGAIN AFTER HOME ALONE
(OR HOME ALONE AFTER SEX AGAIN)

Remember that scene in *Kramer versus Kramer*, where Dustin Hoffman has finally stopped sulking over being chucked by his wife and ventured forth to pastures new? The pastures new tiptoes naked to the loo and bumps inevitably into dad's flatmate – his cute kid. The look on everyone's face is a picture which is, of course, why it got so many Oscars. She looks as embarrassed as if her mother had caught her at it, while he looks blank because his brain hasn't yet been programmed to deal with this kind of thing. The kid becomes all powerful in the face of their dumbness. He takes it all in, then asks her, 'Do you like fried chicken?' Her frozen smile cracks into a reply, 'Why yes!' and she backs off to retrieve her clothes without showing her bum lest she cause further offence.

Not very dignified, and she didn't have to hide. She could have tried a verbal explanation. She could have started with ticking something on her clipboard (always have a clipboard handy whenever you sleep abroad). 'I was just examining your father's bed for some details for the valance measurement. Do you know what valances are, Son?' Perhaps not. If the child registers more than nought on an IQ scale. On the other hand, why the worry? All that's happened is tentative penetration with a new partner, in the absence of the previous one. But because it's so much on our minds, the idea of the perfect family unit, we feel honour bound not to alter it. Are we breaking a taboo by going to pastures new? We are bombarded with news stories about famous people who do it. Are we supposed to feel 'There but for the grace of God' as another weather girl swaps her partner?

But it gets sillier. On the one hand, we are encouraged to re-group and try again for a second nuclear set-up to avoid becoming another awkward statistic and a 'burden to the State', or an 'embarrassment at the school parents' barn dance'. On the other hand, we are told to be responsible about the future generation. We must avoid creating a generation of glue sniffers and latch-key kids. So, if you get lucky with a single parent with children, or they get lucky with you, beware the consequence of terminal derangement in the offspring. (I accept that merely pointing out contradictions in life can get irritating, but who knows when one might get the call to appear on *Question Time*?)

So given that you have gone round and round in circles about the should-I shouldn't-I and what would the child think if she sees me in the nuptial bed with another geezer, you might be inclined at huge cost and months of planning to arrange a babysitter and go out into the night air without your charge. Window shopping for nookie is best done at night – Tesco's and Asda are not good pulling temples in the day time. Although some more enlightened stores are facing up to their responsibilities by providing singles nights for shoppers – 'one plus one', hopefully.

And so, given all the deliberation, one eventually decides to go for it. (You can bet the male equivalent parent doesn't stall as long as this.) My first liaison was only after a friend had pimped the man for me. She said, 'Go on, give him a ring, he's desperate.' (And he was, but not necessarily for me.) Anyway, I finally plucked up the courage to ring, having circled the phone a few times and drunk the vodka. Finally, I slurred, 'Derek?' because that was his name. He said, 'What's up?' I thought, no, this isn't going well. This isn't what you should be saying. You should be saying, 'Helen, at last.' Anyway, we finally made a date. For three months' time, which was mutually acceptable. He suggested the venue, which foxed me at first. I couldn't remember if he'd said 'tea rooms du boisson' or 'tea rooms des Billy'. There were loads of tea rooms in the area and I was too full of vodka to phone him back for clarification. Anyway, I finally found it by following a Cosi Car cab who knew the way. Things are looking up, I thought as I arrived. He has hair! And the date was perfectly agreeable. Not much could go wrong with three bottles of wine each and a side salad.

Anyway, we finally drove home and parked outside my house. He said, 'Well?' and I said, 'Well,' and then he said, 'Well?' and I thought, 'I've got to stop saying this,' so I said did he want to come in for a quick coffee? Well, I didn't actually get to say the word 'coffee', because he was round my side of the car to release my seat belt and then he put his tongue down my throat. Then he said, 'I hope I haven't offended you.' Well! It had been so long since I'd had any sort of physical tonguing whatsoever, I'd forgotten what was offensive and what wasn't! I thought perhaps that's how it's done nowadays? A quick snog and an apology. I was used to the old ways – when we used to say things like, 'Can you move your poncho a bit, the tassles are making me sneeze,' or 'Mind your patent leather clogs, they're digging in rather.' But I thought it doesn't mean I can't adapt to modernism. Because you've got to be aware nowadays, haven't you?

So, we went into the house. I tried to get rid of the babysitter as quickly as possible. Grovel, grovel, Thank you so much for watching the TV, and Oh, I see you finished the biscuits, great! And Oh goodness me, you found the pizza! I hope the sell-by date means it poisoned you! Only joking! Oh. The tonic ran out? And the gin? I *am* sorry . . . Did she wake up at all? Only when you had your orgasm. Oh, I didn't know your boyfriend was coming over? Oh. He didn't. Just you . . . ! Fine! Well, I expect you'll be rushing off. Oh yes, this is my brother, Derek. Now he would run you home but he's not going to. Are you Derek? No, there's no need to give Tina a lift home (you get in that car with that all-in-one legging suit and you're dead), only joking!

She finally left and I thought, right. This is it. He's in my house. The child is upstairs and we're locked in. I'd put the catch up. It's now or never. So I made the obligatory coffee which neither of us drank in case it made our breath smell, and we drank some Baileys, because that was the only alcohol I had left in the house that the babysitter hadn't actually polished off, which made our tongues cleave to the roof of our mouths. So then I did the daring thing. I thought, I've got to make a connection. I mean, all right, he's put his tongue down my throat, but he doesn't really know me. So I arranged my face to look like Michelle Pfeiffer or someone similar in features to me, and said in a little girl sort of voice, 'Would you tuck me in, please?' He said, 'Where?' I said, 'Bed. The bed. Would you tuck me in the bed?' And while he disappeared to the loo I raced upstairs so I wouldn't have to be seen getting into the bed. It's funny, it's the thing I do naturally and unthinkingly every day of my life but, suddenly, in front of someone else it makes me not want to do it. Unless I do it fast they get to see my body, and if I do it slowly I get to see it. Which has to be avoided.

Anyway, eventually he came upstairs and found me under the covers. He asked did I always sleep with my clothes on? I relented, and took off my boots, but I

didn't want to commit myself too much at this stage. And then came the moment.

I said, 'Do you have a thing for doing this with?' because that's what you have to say nowadays, it's the new repertoire. Luckily, he said he did but he'd have to go to the car to get them. I said, 'fine.' He said 'I hope you like them.' I said, 'I'm sure I will.' (Although I was getting more doubtful by the minute.) He said, 'They're a bit old.' I said, 'What?' He said, 'Old. But Lennon and McCartney just don't age do they? They are the best for doing harmonies with.'

I said, 'Oh.' To be fair he had mentioned harmonies earlier on, but I hadn't been concentrating. I was worrying about how to get him into bed and out by midnight, and in that state you agree to most things. Harmonies? Fine. The thing is, I have a problem with harmonies. I can't sing with people I don't know. There's a lot of things I can't do with people I don't know and singing is high on the list. Having to keep your own note while he does the descant. It's so unsexy and it's no good being offered the tune to do because that's just patronising. Anyway, I didn't know what to do. In the end, I got a tube of tomato purée and sort of squidged it over the duvet to fake a . . . you know. It's an old Barbara Cartland trick. It never fails.

The next week I thought, 'No. I've been rash.' I was

listening to the Archers on my own and I thought what would Shula Archer have done in my position? She'd probably have said forget the harmonies, forget the Johnnies, lets get at it! So I arranged another date, this time going back to his house for a 'quick coffee'. While he was in the kitchen making it, I raced upstairs, ripped off my clothes and lay provocatively across his bed waiting for his return. He nearly dropped the sugar bowl he was so startled. I said, 'Do it, do it to me now, this minute.' He said, 'Why this minute?' I said, 'Because my babysitter goes into double time after midnight.' He said, 'What about foreplay?' I said, 'Forget it. I'll settle for two play. You can owe me the rest.' As I said, he was desperate. And so was I. Eventually. I went back to window shopping after that. Never rush in when you can peruse first.

'WHAT ABOUT A DATING AGENCY?' – COMPLACENTLY MARRIED PEOPLE OFTEN SUGGEST THIS

'In this day and age.' This will always be cited in the same breath when expounding the virtues of a dating agency. 'In this day and age.' It is harder and harder to meet people even though, paradoxically, there are more and more of you – therefore it is perfectly reasonable to want to speed fate along a bit and to stem the loneliness.

So I researched door-to-door dating agencies, which are a growth industry and offer results. I thought, great! It'll be instant now. At least I'll get instantly disappointed as opposed to the normal three months. With hindsight, I suppose that if one must look longingly at the classifieds it'd be far better to pick out the hot air balloon section, which is less searing to the heart. This is a good way to get a circumspect view on the world, with some champagne in the basket thrown in. And much nicer than wasting time hanging about hopefully in launderettes, also.

I found my agency at the back of a glossy mag next to an advert for an Audio Tarot Card lady. I couldn't resist her. She read my hand over the phone plausibly enough, although I had to listen very carefully to check that she really *was* turning the cards at her end. She predicted there'd be trouble ahead for me, so she was good in that sense.

The Semen agency was called Personal Select or something like that, with the words 'Bureau' and 'Discreet' and 'Discerning' underlined in pink underneath. Altogether Disastrous, as it turned out. A Mr Personal Select came to my house with a briefcase. Apparently they were short staffed, or were the staff just short, I can't remember? But, anyway, he was very short in a convincing sort of way. On the doorstep he waved a photo at me of his (new) family. This was in lieu of an ID card. As stated I was partly doing this for research – yes, that's right – and partly to pay someone to get me out of the hole I was in. Now, of course, big lesson: *this can't happen*. You have to be ready to get out of your own hole which you may have inadvertently dug for yourself – or have fallen into, depending on your circs.

Anyway, what the man lacked in charismatic authority he made up for with the size of his questionnaire. Fortunately for him I quickly got very bored with it, so I signed away impatiently, thinking we'd get on to the nitty-gritty soon after. The nitty-gritty being, I assumed, a complimentary appraisal of myself complete with a few perfunctory compliments about my personality, looks and general demeanour, with the promise of getting a few dates. As he was there for a long time, droning on about mankind and existential growth, I drifted off and started hallucinating that he was the man who used to sell brushes and tea towels door to door at home in suburbia. He had that kind of voice, like the man who used to do *Mr and Mrs* on daytime telly – very smooth but not listening and therefore quite menacing. I woke myself up from this reverie by shouting 'NO BRUSHES THIS TIME, PLEASE!'

He chose to ignore this by comfortingly saying it can be hard on one's own and would I be prepared to go on the Deluxe Membership? This for three hundred quid more. And what did I get for the Deluxe Membership that I wouldn't get on the ordinary membership, for which I'd just paid £300? Quick as a flash and slightly irritated that I'd asked, he frankly told me that to 'go deluxe' was really the difference between playing at the thing and wasting his time or meaning business.

I can only thank God that I didn't sign up for the Deluxe Nirvana land. Surely coughing up the first £300 should get me just one date, just to see . . . ?

At the end of that chat (almost midnight now, and him hoping for a lift to the station in an agitated sort of way) he concluded that I was reasonably attractive with 'something' to offer . . . I pinned him down on this. It turned out he liked my sofa and generously could not see why other men shouldn't feel the same – he didn't see why there should be a problem. But I had my doubts by then. People who talk in negatives have anal retention and use natural deodorants which don't work. He allowed that having the child might not *necessarily* be a preventative factor in 'partnering up', although he couldn't promise anything because he was a professional and didn't believe in giving false hope.

Having pocketed the cheque, tucked his notes back in his briefcase, and swivelled his trousers around in preparation for standing, he switched off his smile and I agreed that, yes, he really was very professional. But where did he train? Because he was a very, very good fraud. The training of life, he told me. Ah . . .

Rip off, or is my name single parent? I didn't hear from him, surprisingly, so I tried to phone him. I got to hear a plethora of answering machines. Once, I broke through on to his mobile where he assured me he was on a case. The Old Bailey. Thankfully, some less embarrassed clients had reported him. I would have liked to have met these brave clients, we would have a lot to share about him and our ordeal – deluxe or not – and, who knows, we might have gone on to greater things together.

Another useful fact you should know about yourself when presenting yourself as fodder for the dating game, is that just because you're *single* you're not *fancy free*. You don't get to be that twice. Not until you're eighty, and then chances are you'll be too old then to want to party without a babysitter. No. Being single with children involves chains of a different sort. Obviously there is some freedom of movement. I mean, you can still ask a man back to your home, *but only*:

1. If you've paid through the nose for a babysitter to sleep over in the attic with the child and to stay there until given a sign to come downstairs – even if this takes a few days in coming.
2. If there is no evidence of wet-wipes. Men don't use these, ever. If caught, you could say they are special CD cleaners.
3. If there are no crunchy rusks or toasty Marmite fingers in your own bed to interfere nastily with his manhood.
3. If any children's drawings are scattered about you say they are samples for a charity project you're working on.

On a first date, relax, you can be truthful later. A good time is when you want to get rid of him. Or you can let it out bit by bit if you're not sure and need him to erect some shelves for you first. (See barter exchange, Chapter 4.)

The case for resorting to the classifieds is when you need a little help from your friends and they are all out, or on holiday. So, I told myself, 'Widen your net, loosen your pride and look in the classifieds.' I found a PO box number which appeared to offer it all: 'Person required. No police record preferred.' (Having avoided the 'Sexy lady required must be slim for fun 'n' frolics,' it goes without saying.) I turned up at an agreed venue – an Old Yuppie Pubbe – and waited, thinking how nice all the other men looked. They were there for a reason. To highlight the contrast betwixt them and my PO box. He was distressingly ugly, but lucky for him didn't seem to mind. He beamed at me. How did he know it was me? I thought, as I straightened up from stuffing my paper, red rose and name tag into my holdall. Damn. No chance for a runner then.

He liked to guess things about people. I was happy to let him enjoy himself. He was wrong on everything. I guessed right first time. His wife didn't understand him. They had two wonderful kids. The divorce was due any minute and he had a lot to offer. Like what? Travel. Where? Epsom. Been there. There's a very nice bed and breakfast . . . No. Oh . . .

Instead, we went to a restaurant and had to squeeze into a very public window seat for the world and his wife to look in and have a laugh at me with my PO box. He leant across and clasped my hand. Because I am well brought up I smiled pleasantly back and at a convenient moment – the next one – reclaimed my hand to adjust my fringe. When my hairstyle had been given a thorough make-over he reclaimed my hand. I swiftly claimed it back again to adjust my jacket, my napkin, my fork, and yes, my knife. He stopped then.

But let's suppose you do find someone nice; the first cut is the deepest. Once, I forgot rule three about not having left crumbs in the bed – and was only able to offer Pooh Bear plasters. That was OK. Sort of. But the appearance of Baba the Elephant from behind the pillow at the crucial moment stemmed the flow. 'Laughing it off' took supreme effort.

But what can you do? It is worse in my view to sit a man down and say heavily, 'I really feel we have something here, but may I just tell you about me in two ticks before we go any further. I have this wonderful child . . . Oh, bye then . . .' Or sometimes it can have the opposite effect. They get really excited at the news and race upstairs to take a peak. He's got three more like her at home. He's missing them already. Oh, bye then . . .

You can bet the ex won't have to negotiate this stuff. Either his new partner need never find out – he will have had time to hide the odd nappy in between Access visits – or the girlfriend may think it's a cute 'plus' – safe in the knowledge, the child is hardly likely to cut in on their relationship time.

As a final resort, ask the friend who pimped for you last time to host an impromptu meal that you are paying her to have. Ask her to invite a bunch of other strangers, then sit next to the least offensive one and start dating him. You can then claim you met 'at a friend's house'. By far the most socially acceptable and the least challenging.

24

DATING BLIND

There I was. Freshly single again with young child, so I decided to give myself up to being 'a bit of a case'. It was the best excuse I'd had so far in life to do so, and considering I wasn't even able to make finite decisions about which type of toothpaste to use, it seemed authentic enough. I became easily led by others who weren't in the same mess.

I was eventually taken pity on by another parent. This new friend was category NU. 'New and unknown'. Open your eyes, I thought. Give it a go.

We had no shared history, but what the hell? Just because I hadn't known her in my formative years, when I had done things in hedgerows and against walls, shouldn't matter. We couldn't say to each other 'Brittany' in a knowing sort of way and collapse into hysterics, because she hadn't been there. But she had probably done her own 'Britanny', I expect. Or had she? I hoped so, or else our friendship might run aground.

This friend was procured on the nursery school circuit. One day, I plucked up courage and invited her child to tea with mine. It was an event. It was the first child-led tea selected by my own child. I was standing by on my best behaviour out of respect for this new social phenomenon. I tiptoed round the two children, serving them buns, plasticine, glue, wet-wipes – well, I put them out, whatever they commanded, they got. When the mother appeared at six for collection, I knew I had to get into the right mode. But what was it? I surveyed the options. Tea, coffee, wine and whisky. I felt the choice might be burdensome, so I simplified and said, 'Glass of wine?'

She looked shocked. 'No, no. I've got to get back.' She cuddled her child protectively. The coat stayed buttoned up. I could see her eyeing the dressing-up clothes suspiciously. (Some suspenders, an old stained nightie and a jock strap.) She left without even a beverage. I made a mental note not to offer wine next time. You offer a cup of tea which they then decline because they're busy and have places to go. That way, everyone is happy. I know that now, of course. (I washed the jock strap, also.)

Now this friendship could have hit the dust, but because of my first tentative gesture she reciprocated until, would you believe it, this mother controlled my life. Teas, outings and then – seeing that I still couldn't be assertive about which toothpaste to get – she arranged a BLIND DATE. If only she'd come in on my washing, mending and ironing, but I didn't know her well enough for that. I was happy with the prospect of a blind date, though. Another first for me. Like flock wallpaper I thought blind dates were not really my scene – but beggars can't be, and the 'foursome' was arranged.

The only down side was that it had to be held at a dinner dance. I tried to be open minded, but I feared discoing to the Barron Knights more than life itself. So it was with heavy heart that I turned up – partially from dread alone and partially from a late and truculent babysitter who had, I suspect, an eating disorder. (I wouldn't mind, but it's difficult to plan the week's meals with an empty fridge each time you go out.) Anyway, I arrived. I placed myself near the fullest bowl of peanuts and began plucking the hairs from my coat as fast as I could. I stopped when I spotted my new category

NU friend had arrived. With husband a respectful two steps behind. I complimented her on her appearance. She graciously accepted. I waited expectantly for my return compliment, but there was none. She got down to the important business of clearing peanut crumbs, polishing the surrounding seats and miming to the waiters for a J-cloth. I noted that my eclectic semi-gypsy look was at odds with the compulsory black and tan look. I was the odd one out. Unlike her, I just hadn't had time for the high-intensity sun bed, and I said as much. This put a hold on conversation. Then my date arrived. My friend waved frantically and I braced myself. Out of the crush of DJs I saw my designated partner. (Only for the evening I added, to console myself.) As soon as I made out all four foot one of a diminuitive figure engulfed in a DJ, my heart sank. My fault for having any expectations at all, but really – Toulouse Lautrec! Couldn't she have warned me?

Anyway, Toulouse, interestingly enough for him, had suffered a terrible day and he challenged any of us to come up with a worse one. This before we were introduced. My offers of trauma were sensibly dropped as I realised that he had to share *now* or else explode. He told us he had just been chucked by an unreasonable cow. No surprises there, I thought. I sighed and knew with heavy heart that all I had to do was get through the evening. I went to the loo to keep my spirits up. I calculated only five and a half hours to go. I found a magazine in there and tried on all the perfumes, making it four and a half when I came out. They'd given up waiting for me and I had to hunt for them among a blaze of tanned backs and diamanté décoletés. I found Toulouse, who was by now surrounded by three bottles of wine which he wasn't sharing with anyone. He asked me where I'd been. I told him I'd just rung the babysitter. He paused for a milli-second and then said he didn't want to disappoint me but he wasn't 'up to it' tonight. I reassured him that neither was I. Phew, I lightly said, as if joking.

My category NU friends were on the top table. She'd since put on a pair of gloves up to her armpits. I hoped it wasn't a competition for later. Toulouse hadn't heard of the glove game, so I assume it was just a one-off. Anyway I was happier sitting below salt without glove.

Later, Toulouse and myself were invited to see some blue movies while watching the sun come up over Hyde Park. I didn't want to sound ungrateful but I *knew* I was from another planet. I said, 'I feel like Alice! Curiouser and curiouser.'

'Alice couldn't come,' said the new friend's respectful husband. 'That's why we had a spare.'

Oh. How nice to belong to a society where there's always a spare ticket. I wonder why, though?

All around us people were ordering steak sandwiches. As we had just washed down the steak and two veg from the dinner bit of the dance, I worried I might throw up, watching more flesh consumed. I used this as an excuse to leave. Toulouse joined the blue movie pack, saying it was a first for him. Which? The date or the movie? The movie. Apparently, my NU friends were always doing the blind date bit. It was Alice last time. Alice could have warned me if I'd known her to ask. I threw myself on the mercy of the cab rank.

Was it worth it? Yes and no. Now I know never to do a dinner dance. The babysitter waited until I'd tucked myself into bed, relieving the worst moments in my mind, before ringing the bell. She'd forgotten her pants. I handed them to her, shivering in the moonlight. My NU friend's long gloves would have come in handy, after all.

25

BONDING AND BONDAGE

One understanding of 'bondage' is the fear of being tied forever to an ironing board or a sink with hundreds of children clamouring for your attention and no-one around to help you. Or the fear of being stuck in a marriage or partnership whereby you can't psychologically see the wood for the trees and sensibly bugger off.

'Bonding', on the other hand, is where you GET ON VERY WELL with someone. Sometimes too well – whole companies do it to get bigger, and back benchers do it to get on telly. Bonding with one's child takes *less* time and trouble. It is natural. Just as a monkey delouses her chimp or a bird feeds a worm to her baby birds; they are all bonding away. The mother puts in stuff, the mother gets back stuff, and on it goes.

However, if you are a single parent, this natural behaviour, just as in the wild of your kitchen or garden, is often criticised, observed and commented on. It is criticised by Database Collators. They have decided this relationship is more one of *bondage* then *bonding*.

It's easy to spot a database collator by the way. They turn into government ministers so it's best to know what they look like. A typical collator will have gone to Oxford or Cambridge, wear a blazer with gold buttons and corduroys for weekends. Just like his old school uniform, in fact. They are paid a reasonable living wage with membership to the odd club thrown in. And I don't mean

'Water World'. We're talking male establishments, where you get Yorkshire pudding, a discreet de-dandruffing by the commissionaires and a special footrest placed beneath the favoured leather upright. These Boyz have never been young. They skipped the life experience, which is why they are best placed and equipped to collate data. They are picked for the job at seven when they first go to 'Grooming House in Upper Charterhurst'.

For the privilege of rubbing conkers with a few other chaps from Whitehall, these Boyz must slip a few key figures and suppositions into influential articles, and if they prove themselves to be completely divorced from reality, a few White Papers also. Their job is simple. They must demonstrate at all times that 'Single parenting is really rather dangerous and if only everyone was married we'd have no crime'. They must make this easy and logical to grasp. They can do this in various ways. One is to imply through their figures that the 'Quality of relationships found in single-parent set-ups is overly close', thus causing yet more crime, of course.

The Boyz in Blazers may or may not have spoken to single parents in the course of their 'findings', but they have to write it all up in neat. They say that *over-intimacy* and *over-bonding* with one's child is an inevitable consequence of single parenting. They might even steal the line from the odd celeb to give weight. 'Yes, Josh and I are very close,' muses some actress. 'Too close, perhaps?' she is asked. She breaks off and looks into the distance bravely. Well, I wouldn't like to go to *her* coffee mornings, thanks.

I'm surprised the Boyz in Blazers gave weight to such unweighty examples nicked from *Hello!* mag, but on the other hand this has taken over from Hansard as a great source of statistical back-up for most government White Papers. They are asked to worry about popular consent, so need to address what they think public opinion is.

I was reading about some of this research at the same time as having my lowlights put in. I was sufficiently incensed to draw it to the attention of the hairdresser. He was talking about his kitten at the time. (All I said was, 'And how's the kitten?' to start him off, before settling back into my magazine knowing I wouldn't have to speak for some time.) I didn't want to lie about my holidays or other stuff I hadn't got planned. However, he was just on to litter trays with self-regulating faeces training when I gave up and asked his view.

'Look,' he says, firmly whacking a dollop of bleach on to my greys, 'A kitten stays with its mother, yes? He snuggles, he has love-in. Then he goes. Poof! He is loved, so he is independent. Yes?'

The kitten analogy is a useful one, I feel. And one to draw on. 'Exactly!' I said. 'What's unhealthy about forming healthy, independent beings?' I asked. My hairdresser didn't reply. He'd popped out to the hardware store for more bleach. I'm very porous, but I knew we were on the same side.

So, to return to the first tentative definition of bondage: does *bonding* become *bondage*? Here are some exploratory questions to ask oneself if one has a morning free with nothing better to do than worry oneself needlessly.

1. Does closeness in a single-parent household result in an unhealthy codependence (as they say in American football)?
2. Does this slippery slope of love lead to bondage in a bad way?
3. Does the leverage in the love stakes of two parents at once mean the love rations are correctly apportioned? Not too much, and not too little?
4. Do we then deduce that a single parent can't ration her love in the same way, hence destabilising her child?

Help. Have a coffee and carry on into the afternoon if you've still time to get upset.

5. Does the single parent have an overspill of love because it can't be directed at another live-in grown-up, and hence give off too much loving to child?
6. So is *that* why we need two parents at once in the same house? To make sure the child doesn't get *too much* love and attention *at once*?

Otherwise, that child may well feel deprived of the correct amount of love, which is less than his nuclear cellmates are getting. He'll go home and beg to be loved less. He'll complain to his probation officer. 'I was loved too much as a child, that's why I did it. It was to get less attention.'

I see. Well, the world knows best. That's why we have this view in magazine and legal form.

You know what they say. The lower the self-esteem, the higher the conformity. I didn't know this but heard about it on *Kilroy*. With this in mind I went to Pet City near Willesden, as advised by my hairdresser, and bought a kitten to add weight to my case. And basket. I wanted to see if a kitten could flourish in a single-parent household. I hoped it would not become too intense with me and set up expectations I couldn't fulfil. I needn't have worried. Once the cat flap was in place the kitten came and went as it pleased. Balanced, happy and independent. Kitty had the courage to investigate the world but the thought of its happy home enticed her back.

However . . . it's not all independence and light. If you're worried about when the next job is coming in, the toast is burning, the child is innocently yelling, the video is showing mindless violence at odds with its innocuous cover and you can't get near the TV to switch if off because you're trying to control the

ironing . . . yes, one would feel intensely tied. And resentful of your lot. That day.

You might well think, I do *all* this, yes *all* this. I fold the tea towels, I get the Jif mousse in, I read the homework, I wake when she does at five a.m., and *he* strolls in with a talking Baby Born or a Polly Pocket, complete works, and gets the glory.

Yes, one feels a touch possessive when, unusually tired and pimply, one glimpses the new girlfriend who has bonded magnificently with one's child. Being young and ambitious and richer than me helps make it nasty. Apparently, 'Caro' took a thermos of coffee to the fair. I want to say, 'Now what kind of person takes a thermos to a fair? How sad. Is she fifty? Or just mean?' Instead, one says 'Great!' with a pang so strange it tears you apart.

In the land of cats, it's all sorted. Territory, coupling, offspring, community boundaries – the lot. No punishing labels to deal with in the jungle. You mate. You fight. You win or lose, and you survive.

People, on the other hand, are more confused. God knows how those data collators would survive without their Yorkshire pudding or favourite armchair. Hang on. An idea has been born – out of wedlock naturally. How long is it till next Guy Fawkes night . . . ? No-one would ever know it was me . . .

26

THERE ARE NO GUARANTEES

Once you are separated you will be bound to notice that, while your child is most definitely your pride and joy, this same child is most certainly fifty per cent part of the other parent also. Unless it's a test tube or other origin, which would cut down any bother one hundred per cent. A tube can't demand to be consulted about piano lessons, for instance.

For the rest of your life you may have to endure a difficult relationship with the other fifty per cent shareholder who is likely to claim his dividend – sometimes in ways which may be at odds with you. You have to let this happen. Even though you may never know if she cleans her teeth there, eats too many sweets there, gets terrified at *Bambi*, snuggles up with the new girlfriend. That's not your percentage area.

Or it all may be marvellous. No need to read on then.

Every partnership is different. (I know. This amazes me, also.) But there does seem to be a common denominator that links most separations – unhappiness. Even though time heals, no amount of it will completely get rid of that sinking feeling when you have to communicate with the seed donor – that sense of depression when having to, however briefly, chat with that now foreign person. But give yourself a break. This is understandable. You liked each other once, after all. Well, you must have for at least thirty seconds. (Mother Nature works fast.) There are no tricks to make this mode of conduct becoming. Or I would have found out about them by now.

Of course, there are some ecstatic step-families who pride themselves on the perfection of their estrangement arrangements. They have newsletters, away weekends, and even get to drop in on telly when there's a gap for voyeuristic, 'amazing yet moving' stories about families.

If you know any such professionally divorced people, as I do, you will be told how the divorce was really the best thing. The parents are now best friends, the children are flourishing and, in some tidy cases, divorced couples marry other divorced couples and, hey! All the kids party every day. It's a riot. Apparently.

The ecstatics omit to tell you about the dark hours they had before another available divorcee came by, saving them from loneliness and despair. That is not for public consumption. But family symmetry is. It's something to shout about. The louder you shout – the lonelier you once have been. Still, mine's not to reason. It's too late for that. Mine is to get on with it.

And then, of course, there are those men who never 'feel' in the first place. They were never taught how to by their repressed 'stay-together-at-all-costs' nuclear parents, and so a parting of the ways is no more mentally challenging than getting together was in the first place. They are blessed in some ways. No emotion. And it's no good saying, 'But look what they are missing,' because they are not missing much. Lots of crying and feeling cross is not something anyone should covet. I can't decide which is more ghastly: born-again, estranged or emotionless know-alls.

I opt for the 'just do the best you can' mode, and forgive myself for getting it wrong sometimes. Estranged, hurt people who have only the love of their mutual child in common, do and will continue to behave badly and think nasty thoughts at times. And although there's no great dignity in this, at least, somehow, practise makes it more familiar and you get better at conning the world into a state of 'courtesy'. Like a visit to the post office or bank. Some marriages are founded on this principle, so there's no difference, except you don't share the bills.

I find it useful, after a difficult bout of access exchanges, to do something extra nice. It might be a Saturday morning, but Cointreau and slimline tonic have to be tried. And if this feels too indulgent, invite someone round for a bout of sex – anything to make you forget the hundred yesterdays when neither of you got it right. And you can rest assured someone else in the United Kingdom is mixing their drinks or experimenting with bed linen just like you.

AND NOW THE OVERVIEW

There are no winners in estrangement. Only estrangement. But, looking back, without that original but flawed connection, I would have no child, and for me that would have been complete loss. A child is the ultimate joy. A child is better than sex – even though they're close.

All around is the notion that the better child is the one born and raised in a nuclear family with two practising, sexually communicative parents. (Not too much, mind, but a discreet diaphragm hidden in the bathroom cabinet would be acceptable to the treasury.)

OKEY DOKEY

So how can we explain the fact that some of these blessed children also become unfocused, unloving, under-achieving, or even law-breaking members of society just as children from single-parent homes do?

Who's to say a nuclear beginning generally guarantees creating an acceptable human being, and that a single-parenting beginning generally will not? Where are the statistics on this?

Marriage? Living arrangements? Under whose roof each parent abides at any given time? Are these the parameters by which to judge, assess and explain our troubled new generation?

All you can hope is that by experiencing love from the beginning, no matter how many roofs the parents have lived under at any given time, the child will be loving, optimistic, and enjoy a laugh.

To turn roof-top arrangements and income levels into the Plimsoll line of good and bad people is . . . unpersuasive. Of course, we all have bad days – in my case years – but it's not necessarily your income level or your roof-top status that sends you into a decline.

The most important thing to consider is the future generation. Will they be kind, informed and confident? And if they – *quelle horreur* – stem from a single-parent unit, who will give a toss? Will they be penalised because they didn't have married parents when they are running the Bank of England, or Channel 4, or being flourishing individuals? Will they be refused a passport, or disqualified from the workplace because their parents were divorced, separated, widowed or not married ever?

No.

The important thing is forgiveness. Forgive yourself. Forgive the bastard who got you into this mess. Forgive your lovely child who one day might forgive you – with any luck.